GOD, RELIGION AND POLITICS

GOD, RELIGION AND POLITICS

SUDHA RAMAVAT

Notion Press

Old No. 38, New No. 6
McNichols Road, Chetpet
Chennai - 600 031

First Published by Notion Press 2017

ISBN 978-1-946515-49-0

Dedication

It's very normal and natural that to identify God, humans have created religion. Later on when many religious groups were formed, to express their superiority over other groups, human societies started polluting religion with politics. It's important to find a solution to find peace amongst all different human societies.

Dedicated to humanity worldwide.

Poem by
Rabindranath Tagore

'Go not to temple'

Go not to temple to put flowers upon the feet of God,

First fill your own house with the fragrance of love and kindness.

Go not to temple to light candles before the altar of God,

First remove the darkness of sin, pride and ego, from your heart....

Go not to temple to bow down your head in prayer,

First learn to bow in humility before your fellow men.

And apologize to those you have wronged.

Go not to temple to pray on bent knees

First bend down to lift someone who is down trodden,

And strengthen the young ones.

Not crush them.

Go not to temple to ask for forgiveness for your sins

First forgive from your heart those who have hurt you!

Preface

I believe that our universe is guarded by a super power who is alert every moment. He Manages every activity here, however small or big they are. The extension of this power is present in all the living and nonliving bodies of the universe. We as living beings are able to recognize the presence of the part as our conscious or soul. We as humans can identify it more because we are provided with a very well developed and advanced sensory system. Even the other animals and vegetation also have it, but probably not as advanced.

This super power which is responsible for creation, destruction and overall maintenance of everything here does it very efficiently, but I doubt that He could be bothered about every single being in this universe. He does take care of all in a very perfect way but he has provided us with our souls as his extension, so that we manage ourselves rightly. Of course our conscious is guided and guarded by the unseen guarding hands who help us to move according to our own ability. There are many justified or unjustified excuses we may come out to explain in our favour, that, why we could not achieve a particular goal in life, but the fact remains that we do not get what we do not deserve.

Our Super power "The God" is very closely associated with nature. I feel that He always uses nature to discipline every thing around. Hence go against nature and you get the punishment. Individually or as a group, it does not make the difference. If there is any excess against nature, there is bound to be a reaction we may not like. It can be disastrous. A big natural disaster too. These natural disasters created fear in human mind! A fear of God! Clearly stating that if there is any thing wrong done by any one he has to pay the price for it.

This fear lead people to form groups and have a disciplined life, the philosophy of religion was born in this way.

In the long run with many different groups idealizing different concept of God and the methods to please Him. Religions changed their faces and became politically influenced. This was the most dangerous metamorphosis of faith. Unfortunately it is still going on. As humans we are not happy unless there is some disturbance in the world. Religions in The name of God provides it!

This is a very unhappy situation for a common man who wants to have security, peace and happiness in his family. Actually if he analyses his thoughts properly he has very little to do with God and religion. If he is able to earn enough to supply for the basic needs of his family, he is usually a satisfied person. This is not very satisfactory situation for stalwarts of religious politics. They want more people as followers and more crowd to obey them and fan their ego.

They do not hesitate to threaten people on the name of God or try and misguide the ones who come in contact with them.

Any religion should be regarded as an individual's faith and should be guarded as a private affair of the family they belong to this is my personal opinion. As far as possible those who force themselves and use religion as a means of fooling ordinary people should be treated as untouchable, giving them any importance always causes trouble.

Another important issue in this matter of religion is that as people belonging to a particular nation, it becomes our primary responsibility to maintain our nationality and the prestige of our nation as our prime duty. We should not and we should never flaunt our religious preference publicly. We should always treat our nationality as our first preference and should be kept even above religions. Ref Swami Ram Teerth.

Unless we learn to treat our selves with respect, we can not expect others to treat us properly We should treat our God as our personal friend and guide and the same way religion should be regarded our very own and close to our heart. We should under any circumstances not let it get politically publicized. this will definitely avoid communal disharmony and lead to more peace.

There have been almost forty six old civilizations in this world, during last thousands of years. Roman. Greek, Egyptian, Mesopotamian, Chines, Indian Persian to name a few. Out of all these only one has continued to exists to date and that is Indian civilization. The only reason I can think for Indian civilization to survive so long is the deeply ingrained method of living or their way of life. Hindus as a race belonging to Hindu religion are very patient and tolerant society their faith is like breath of fresh air for them. They do not believe in conversion. Their understanding tells them that if you are born in a Hindu family you are a Hindu, if you are born in a family with some other religion, then that is your faith. Try and understand it and you will find all the answer to all your questions through your religion, about the way you want to look at and find your God. Hence the ways adopted by people of other religions to covert Hindus could not succeed fully and completely. There has been conversions of Hindus to Muslims and Christian faith. These might have been need based or forced, but even those who got converted could not leave their Hinduism altogether. A Hindu may never go to any temple or never pray to any God, but will always remain a Hindu if he wants to and will be treated like one by the followers of Hinduism. Being Hindu did not make any one not to respect and adjust to people of other religion. They accepted all with love and affection and learnt to live together. I have seen the changing attitude of Hindus in present society. To me this appears to be a warning signal. I am also unhappy about the terrorizing activities of Islam. To me it appears that some of the people are trying to demonize it. This is leading our beautiful planet into a battle field. I honestly hope for a better solution before total destruction.

1

———◆———

Almost any time I think about God, my mind refuses to accept him as belonging to any particular religion. At the same time when I hear or read things about any religion and people trying to impose their ideas about God in relation to any other religion I can't accept it as a sensible explanation. This has forced me to analyze my feelings and thoughts in relation to these two entities, God and Religion for my own understanding.

Talking about 'The God' I always think that rather than accepting the God as an eternal, omnipresent authority, it is better to think about him as an overpowering, strong emotional feeling we human beings need for our own protection and preservation. It's easy to think of someone as more powerful and capable than us as a friendly and kind individual. So we like to think that God Is kind, considerate and very caring. To live under an umbrella which can do that to us and let us live the way we want is an ideal situation. If God provides that to us, He is loving and comfortable individual, anybody would love being cared by him. So as humans we have created that loving caring and protecting coverage around us and have him with us always. We have not seen him but felt his presence everywhere around us, so we say he is omnipresent. Our feelings about him direct us to interpret that he cannot be destroyed, so we call him eternal and strong. Someone having all these qualities is there for us. So we start worshipping him and call him God. In my own mind I feel that if there is an authority which is there to give me all the love, protection and security, it's the strength of my mind, which is there to direct me always. Hence I call it a strong emotional strength. Never failing and eternal, present everywhere and in every body so omnipresent.

There is a very strong force existing in nature, which guides it at various levels and regulates its functioning in a very disciplined way. The fact that we are part of this nature and are supposed to be guided, cared protected and disciplined by this force of nature can't be denied, I personally equate this also to God. At the same time, I also feel that the God need not be troubled for taking care of every aspect of our lives. He can't do it, instead we ourselves should work on our own strong emotion in our mind and look after our personal problems on our own. To develop a sense of justice, a sense of right and wrong can really take us very close to a pleasant and peaceful life.

When I was a child, my concept of God was different. I thought of God in terms of images I saw, the statues of various God i.e. Shri Ram, Shri Krishna, Shri Mahadev or Shri Ganesha and Shakti floated in my mind. It provided a lot of strength and solace to me whenever needed. The reason was simple, being born and brought up in a family of Hindus I could draw my strength from these deities. Personally I do not find anything wrong in this. It's like a small child in difficulty, immediately thinks of his or her mother to help him and come out of the trouble he or she is facing. A helping hand, and to many of us our deities provide that. The images of my Gods have not faded in my mind, whenever I close my eyes and offer prayers, I have someone ready to receive, this gives me lot of peace words can't describe. Then the question arises, that should we, who see our God (the strong emotion overpowering the mind) as human figures or to go a step further and see Him in anything living or nonliving, which gives us some pleasure or helps making our survival easy and pleasant, be treated as retarded beings?. After centuries of analysis, thinking and understanding our ancestors found that to control protect and care for self and everything around. We have to learn to combine the emotional force of human mind and the force of nature and identify it as God. Since we are part of nature and consider ourselves to be the best creation of it, who can think emote and govern ourselves and the environment around us, we concluded that if our Godly emotions are to be given a form we have to find it around us only, this led us humans to identify God in everything we can see, touch and feel as representing God. The most intelligent strong caring individuals of the time were gradually identified as godly figures, messengers, prophets and children of God or God himself.

Our ancestors were able to identify the intelligence of the living and nonliving bodies of nature. They admired the Sun for its capacity to convert day into night and night into day. Thus providing the segment of time for working and resting separately. The sun is known to provide energy and make life possible in the world. So it earned the right to represent God and be worshiped.

For time immemorial it has been knowing and observed, that without Sun life cannot exist. To make ordinary person understand this, the wise man in the past created many stories. It was a very interesting story I heard from my grandmother. She used to say, That Mother Nature had two sons, The Sun and The Moon. Since Sun has been allotted the duty of dividing twenty-four hours cycle into two parts, he is provided with a chariot of light driven by horses who are rained by sun rays. Early morning the Sun gets up in his house and rides his chariot and starts his round of the Mother Earth. He always travels from east to west because he has his house on the eastern side of heaven. He makes a full circle of earth from front to back, goes from the west side to his home in heavens to rest.

In the evening when the Sun goes to rest, there is darkness on the earth. This darkness to be reduced and the environment has to be prepared for the creatures of the world in a way so that they can rest and sleep. So the mother calls her other son to take over the duty of creating a soothing cool and comforting atmosphere for the living beings, so that they can sleep, refresh and get ready to face another morning with the rising Sun. The other son of Mother Nature, known as Moon. He is opposite to Sun in everything including looks, habits and nature.

Where Sun is hot, energetic, and quick on taking actions, Moon is cool pale soft and easygoing. The life on earth will become very difficult and almost impossible, if these two brothers do not take their duties seriously. So as the most important residents of earth, it is our duty to keep them happy by wishing them and praying to them regularly every day.

Result was that every day with sunrise we were woken up to wish the sun in a way called Surya Namaskar. It meant that we stood facing east, and let the sun rays fall on our face and body, while folding our hands to say Namaskar to him in prayer form. As the evening turned to night we had to again face towards west and wish and welcome Moon.

The story of Sun and Moon gave so much boost to our imagination. We appreciated the hard job they were allotted by the nature, and were very happy to put them in the category of devas, the Surya Dev and Chandra dev.

The transformation of these planets. And the nature's other gifts I.e. The rain, The Earth, The Sky Light. The other Stars and many such living and nonliving things present in nature were introduced to us as useful and important members of Mother Nature's brigade. They were to be respected loved and cared for if we wanted our life to be happy and pleasant.

Later on when physical geography and science was introduced in the school and I became familiar with the facts, though I became better informed knowledge wise, The Sun still remained Surya Dev and The Moon Chandra Dev. Such was the effect of brain wash during early childhoods.

Eating drinking sleeping and procreation and birth, these activities of nature which appear to be miraculous, which could not be explained easily, but were present around us in the nature. Nature itself was thought of as having great powers to govern lives and was found related to something miraculous and essential. To keep their harmony with life and our need for survival we started pleasing and praying it. Thus we identified God. It's the most easy and natural act of mind.

To me all the things, living or nonliving, present around us, which we see feel and observe, are to be treated with respect, and should be treated as supportive of the strong overpowering emotion we appreciate as God. Whom we cannot see but feel by virtue of being present around us. So to sum up, I believe in that force which makes the universe function properly and our minds to behave in a sensible way. I will like to be a humble supporter of this attitude in people of a similar thinking including myself as God. Ones, while I was working in Libya, my students tried to corner me on this issue. They laughed at me and asked, Dr is it true that in your religion you people worship Dogs, Cats, Stones, Trees and many such things as God? My answer was yes, we do. They laughed. Sarcastically at me and tried to make fun of my belief. I smiled at them sympathetically and told them "this is the difference between you and me, that you don't see him anywhere but I see him everywhere. We did not talk religion after this. I do not want to get a pat on my back because of what I did. I simply mean to convey to all whom I relate to, that our belief and our faith is a creation of our own understanding, no one is capable of challenging it, if we ourselves understand this clearly.

2

There are many instances to prove that human mind has tremendous capacity, to understand, express, and execute whatever it wants. When I am saying human mind I do not want to forget the capacity of other animals who use their intelligence to express their thoughts very successfully.

My grandmother, when she realized that her end was close, decided to do Gau-Dan. (donation of a cow) we had a cow named 'Lachho' whom she selected for the purpose. First she went to our cowshed and talked to Lachho about it, she told her that when she dies and goes towards heaven, she requested that Lachho help her to cross Vaitarny. Vaitarny is the river to be crossed to reach heavens. She gave her reason to Lachho for giving her away as donation to Brahmin. After few days grandmother passed away. We all missed her. The rituals for her peaceful journey started, on the last day when many people were coming to pay their respect, Lachho also came, she stood at our front door, and I have never seen animal shedding tears like she did. Her sorrow did not need any language for expression. That was the first time I understood the impact of forceful emotions. I prayed for the peaceful mind for Lachho that day! I realized the presence of emotions in animals too. More than anything else I understood the reason why we believe that all living beings also have soul (atma). The part of Paramatma.

I remember another friend of our childhood. He was a small dog of silky Sidney breed. We included him in all our playtime activities. He was named Sheru. Sheru was our play mate, protector and a very affectionate companion. I could say that we felt a very good bonding with him. He was capable of emoting successfully. He was very particular about his place to sit, eat or sleep. He never tolerated anyone trying to change his priorities about these. I saw him get angry and chase his friend dog Moti out of the house for trying to impose himself at any of these places, which rightfully belonged to him. Observing his behavior none of us labeled him as selfish, he was very sensible, when any one of us got sick, Sheru was asked to sit and watch. He most dutifully sat near the sick person, made noise if anybody tried to disturb the suffering person, not only that if the person concerned needed some help or care, he ran to call our mother or father or whoever was available. When we were upset and sad about something, Sheru offered his shoulder to cry on. He had no selfish motive in doing this; he only wanted happiness all around him. I equate it to Godliness.

There was another friendly family dog we had while we were working in Libya. He was called Pooch. One family was leaving the country they wanted A familial atmosphere for their dog; we came to know about him through advertisement on the school board. Pooch joined our family by developing mutual liking for each other. Since I was the one for most of the work at home like cleaning feeding, and looking after him, we became great friends. It was his habit to come toward my bed room early in the morning and wake me up, so that I open the door for him to go out. He was very particular about following me, everywhere in the house. Pooch would come and sit near me always as a watchful guard. He used to get very angered if he felt that someone was talking to me rudely. When I would go for bath he used to sit in front of bathroom door He was conscious about timing, if he felt I was taking a longer time than usual he would knock at the door and make sure that all was well.

When I used to take my car out for going to work, Pooch expected that he gets a joy ride in the car before I leave, if I did not give him ride he would not let me go. He used to sit near the kitchen door in the morning and wait for the taste of the breakfast, if he did not get it he very quietly come near me and put his foot on mine to remind me of my forgotten duty. If both of us went out leaving kids had home, he proved to be a good baby sitter.

There was no lacking in intelligence with these animals with which I came in contact in my life. They did not lack in showing that they cared and loved us well. They expressed their emotions and feelings very well even without speaking. I have learned to treat them all with due respect and love. Feeling secured and protected in their company makes me feel that they acted as hands of God.

Then there was this person, a poor rickshaw puller. Bechu engaged by my mother to take our family members wherever they wanted. He used to park his vehicle in front of our house and wait. When nothing important was there, then too he waited in case he could be of some use. My mother was particular that if someone is doing this favor for her, his needs are to be taken care off, as that of any other members of the family. When holidaying at my parents place, this used to be blessing for my kids. Bechu was always there to take them around sometimes for ice cream or otherwise just for roaming. Bechu never complained, my children never felt lack of entertainment. Affection flowed unrestricted. I do not know what my mother paid him, but Bechu's devotion to our family's needs never felt short. I have not been able to place these feelings in their rightful place, but have tremendous respect for Bechu as a fellow human being. He was full of compassion.

I was a very well protected child for my parents. They did not allow me many liberties I wanted. Travelling with my friends was one of them. So once I decided to give my family a shock by giving proof for my ability to be Independent. Few of my friends were going home for a short holiday. They were going in the same direction as my home town; hence I joined the gang, to travel with them. The train used to reach my home town early morning about 4. 30/5am. Reaching the station I took a rickshaw to drive me home. When I got down at home and put my hand on the door bell, to my surprise the door was opened before my pressing It. My father was there to receive me with a very worried expression. He only said "never do such a thing again. His pain and worry made me feel extremely guilty, I promised to take care in future, and we achieved a new dimension to our relationship. Such is the power of emotional power, my father who loved and cared so much for us, got an automatic insight to our minds.

Some times while in a crowd you help some disabled person by guiding him or her to safe place. He or she feels very happy and obliged but does not know you personally. This disabled Person narrates the incidence to a friend and says "I felt as if God himself came to help me." My question is about the feeling which was shared with a friend, do we just put it in a category of an ordinary emotion or think of it as a strong emotion 'The Godish! 'There are so many of this type of incidences we witness and call them miraculous. Do these miracles strengthen our faith in God or humanity or both? People who think like me will say its both humanity and God. An act of help or bravery when done under much needed circumstances is generated in the mind by both.

I wonder what prompted Mother Teresa to come to India to take care of the poor and sick people. A person born and brought up in a foreign land came all the way to India and settled here for good. Her work was exemplary, she came from Macedonia. Daughter of not very rich parents, she lost her father when she was only eight. Her mother was a great influence in her life, whatever they had was always shared with the needy.' We all are related to each other,' was the understanding she got from her mother. Love is the most prestigious gift of life and we must share it with everyone around was her policy. Her devotion to look after poor and sick oozed out so much concern and sympathy to make people comfortable was amazing. She believed she was working for God and devoted herself to the mission she was promoting and taking care of. With the ideology based on love care, and compassion she was instrumental in laying down the foundation of "Missionaries of charity." when you have a chance to look at her photographs her expression is so much full of concern and passion to relieve the suffering from their pain. She naturally springs out as a person with Godly qualities of love and care. Whenever I look at her photos or read about her or think of her, I get great pleasure and happiness by being living on the same planet and same country at the same time as her. It's like sharing my residence with God. OH it's so fortunate! To be able to see God personified!

I do not want to categories my concept of God, belonging to any religion or faith. I also feel that if I say I do not want to feel obliged for following any particular religion, I do not become a nonbeliever. According to me I have a very strong feeling in my mind, which forbids me to do any wrong, to speak lies for my selfish benefits, to go out of my way to harm anyone. And to set on a target to take revenge from somebody without justifying the cause and motives of the person concerned. For me this is my religion, which keeps me closely related to my God and I am happily satisfied with it. It would be very wrong to say that I want every one whom I know, to follow my understanding about The God and religion, but is it too much to think that all of us humans should have a proper understanding about our own perception of right and wrong, and practice our thoughts only by ourselves without imposing them on others?. It's shocking to hear someone saying that, you should perform a particular religious ritual without having anything to eat or drink; otherwise it will not be accepted by God. Or if you face south and not face east for performing a pooja it will go waste. My mind refuses to accept a God so ridged, to not to accept the offerings of a simple minded person simply because he or she did not adapt a typical routine or posture or time. This practice of performing religious rituals in a prescribed notified form is so common amongst Hindus. There are some fanatics, who really believe about wearing a particular outfit or offering particular flowers or particular eatables to God while doing pooja. The charm and pleasure of trying to create a pleasant atmosphere gets totally lost, when such things happen.

Only if we can convince ourselves that the almighty, omnipotent and omnipresent God who takes care of everyone and everything resides in our own mind and guides us to react in a way we think right. Any ritual or methods of paying our respect is entirely our own preference and privilege. Anybody belonging to whatever religion or sect has no right to interfere with that. I might appear harsh in this particular expression, but it is an important feeling to me, to be secured and comfortable in my own methods of communications with my God. And this should be true for all.

3

In Hindu religion, when we talk about God, there is one whom we call the creator the creator is further identified as Nirakar (nirgun) , and the second sakar (sagun) these are worshiped as Brahma. Bramha is also known as lord of creation. We believe that everything in this universe is created by him.

The second God is called the lord of destruction; because everything created has to be destroyed. the God of destruction is called Mahesh.

The third God who is a protector maintainer and an administrator of the universe is called Vishnu. Vishnu usually comes to help those who are facing difficult situations.

The simple reason for describing the God in these various forms could be that the sentiments or emotions which exist during these different activities are different in the mind of the Individual. So let us realize that while engaged in an activity concerned with creation, the state of mind is very different then it is at the moment one is deciding to destroy it. Similarly the mind remains in a different frame when it is trying to impose a disciplinary rules and methods to progress while doing something for maintaining a particular situation for the purpose of constancy and smoothness.

The three strong processes are important to bring out a smooth harmonious environment for the nature to work efficiently. They might be found existing in one mind but at different moments. To put a clear picture about doing three activities differently with precise success and efficiency, the mind is described as three different persons.

There are innumerable stories, which describe the bad to suffer and good to win in battles between God (devas) and demons (rakshasas). The stories are fascinating and act as great food to one's imagination. The main drawback of these mythological stories is that we, as believers start thinking that for all our troubles we have to pray to God and He will come in some form or arrange someway to relieve us of the miserable situation. Many times we take our Dear God so much for granted that even before putting in an effort to put right in place of wrong, we start praying God to do something to rectify the situation. The actions like this leads to disasters many times.

For example, there was a couple, whose son got very sick, instead of rushing him for treatment, they visited Temples, held prayers and pooja at home, the mother fasted and the father visited The Godman The child's condition did not improve instead it deteriorated. By the time they realized that the God will not be able to help, it became too late for the doctor also to do anything. Sadly the child died. The mother was in shock. She could not understand why God did not listen to their prayers, and poojas. she lost faith! I saw this happening, and being a child myself at that time, I could not understand why she had stopped her poojas and prayers. Only later I could remember the incidence, and analyze that sheer ignorance and blind faith In God lead them to so much pain and misery.

The origin of this blind faith lies in the stories of miracles performed by God to save the devotees from various illnesses, economic setbacks, failures in business, misbehavior of spoilt children are many such problems for which people seek God's help through visiting famous religious places like temples and majars or churches and gurdwaras. If they find direct approach is not feasible then the God man are contacted. In such cases the solutions of the problems having sorted out are either fifty fifty, or time based. If God man are experienced enough, they make their profits and leave the victims happy satisfied and hopefully as a regular visitor for them. Otherwise the victim becomes smart and leaves them for good without creating any problems for them. Under any circumstance the shopping of the faith material does not stop.

It becomes a very easy way to fool people and prosper materialistically for the person who is cunning and does not hesitate to become deceitful. Little effort to put on a wise saint's expression, typical clothing and makeup is good enough to fool. Such people are good in sensing the visitor's problems and experts in offering their help with proper soothing language. Dramatic expressions are their speciality, will to be impressed, they can judge by experience. With a little effort they become masters of crowed collection. Rest of the journey as a God man becomes a child's play to them.

On the follower's part people who are stressed by personal and familial problems are present in every part of the world and in every society. They are the best and most profitable targets. Manipulation through the touts and playing on the psychology of the sufferers is a game to be played with caution but that's not a difficult situation for con-man to handle. There are many of these pseudo saints, and many people waiting in world's arena to be fooled.

There was one Professor of psychology who was a best conman one could come across. He resigned from his job when he realized that there are batter opportunities for him, if he becomes a God man, to be able to live in luxury and enjoy his life. After some time he appeared in different attire befitting his new profession. He was a good orator, was good in English and Hindi languages, he was very good in crowed pulling. Within a short time he became famous for his speeches both in Hindi and English. Next step for him was to open ashram where he could take his followers as residents, and train them in the art of enjoyment and reckless liberties. Free use of sex and drugs became his ashrams specialty; huge crowds of people from business class, film industry and politics were attracted by his oratory, freedom and offers of so easily available facilities of dubious nature.

After getting his hands full by the crowds of India, he decided to experiment his expertise in foreign land. He managed to migrate to USA. He opened his ashram there. As he had expected he had success in the form of many followers.

The stories of miracles performed by him were circulated by his touts, amongst the people. The blind folded and the ignorant are found everywhere. And this pseudo saint Prospered.

This God man had a heavenly stay in U S A. People in western countries have good capacity to give costly presents in the form of jewelry cars, electronic gadgets etc. He got a spacious ashram constructed with all luxuries and gave people what they wanted. The unfortunate part for him was that his illegal activities started being noticed by law and governing authorities. So when it was proved that he is harmful to their society, he was asked to leave. By this time he had caught up with age, also his own ambition and inclination towards harmful activities in life, created health problems. He came back to die in India!

My self-had an experience, when my son passed his grade twelve, and started looking for future opportunities. He for some reason underwent depression. I could not find any way to cheer him up. He stopped talking and communicating. As his mother I was stressed and could not think what I could do to make him comfortable and easygoing as before. During this period my restlessness and worry faltered my sensibility. I was prepared to do anything for my son, to get him back was my only thought and aim. One day a pundit came to my home declaring that he was directed by one of my friend to talk to me and help me find a solution. The pundit asked for his Janam patri (astrological description depending on the time date and place of birth of the individual). He asked some questions about my son, then he did some calculations. Finally with a very serious, glum face he told me that my son's fate is very heavily affected by Rahu. If some precautions are not taken he can suffer a lot, he might even try to end his life. I was in shock; it was the darkest day of my life. I could not think anything; I felt that my world has come to an end. Looking at my face pandit ji adapted a sympathetic attitude, he promised to help and improve the situation, he said I will have to do mahamritunjaya path. I agreed immediately. Which mother will not?? Ultimately the path was arranged two more pandits joined, we performed the pooja, my son and my daughter both joined me in the temple.

As an after effect of this pooja I cannot claim that things improved immediately. I felt little better and hoped my son will have a better out look of life. Pundit ji had given him a holy thread, to be tied on his wrist, and a Tabeez to be put in a black thread round his neck. Psychology played its role; we felt all is well for the time. Doing pooja was good. As time passed I realized that my son's attitude changed, he became totally dependent on the holy thread around his wrist, and the Tabeez round his neck. He would get very uncomfortable if any one of these were not on him. By this time I had gotten over my fears, and was able to analyze my own feelings which could have inspire this weakness in my sons behaviour. I realized how important it is for an adult, specially a parent to keep his or her emotions under control in challenging situations. We talked and I tried to bring him out of his fear, that if he is not wearing his charms he is going to suffer. It took a very long time for him to get over this dilemma. I learnt from this experience that our source of confidence in self is in the faith that our strong emotional strength is in our minds. That is our individual God. We should never ignore this if want to save ourselves from calamities caused by blinding ourselves by pressurizing circumstances.

When my thoughts delve on the Hindu concept of Brahma, Vishnu, and Mahesh, it seems that these are the various forms of energy sources, which are created in the mind according to our requirement. According to our needs and physical environment they change the nature and direct us to behave as needed, even when we call ourselves belonging to a particular religion. The notion we hold as God, is a creation of our own mind. We see him as we want. I.e. if I want to think Ram as God, in my imagination the person who appears is wearing traditional clothes he is seen in his statues I have seen in temples or pictures or as in the serials or movies made on Ramayana. I do not find any other concept of Bhagwan Ram more appealing to my senses. Same is the case when I think about Christ, or Guru Nanak Dev., when thinking about Allah, no particular image comes to my mind, for the simple reason that I have not seen a Muslim God. The only image which comes to my mind when thinking about Muslim God is their place of worship The Mosque. If same is the thought processing of normal average persons like me, then I am more than certain about what I feel 'God' is Correct.

Talking about Ram who is supposed to be the incarnation of Vishnu, he was born as a human to kill the demon king Ravana.

It was the destiny of Ram who was incarnation of Vishnu. In this world the simple rule is that if you are born, there can't be any other way to complete the journey of life but dying. All we do in our life is guided by the circumstances. These circumstances are creation of our destiny. Now the question springs up is 'what is destiny'. The answer to this query is that it is an unwritten statement of whatever is going to happen in the life for us or whosoever's destiny we are talking about. For all of us it is said that our karma (way we lead our life) decides what we have to face in life. Meaning that if we have lead a life always doing right and proper activities have never harmed any one, never hurt anyone, we can have a good life. The difficulty arises at this juncture. Can we always judge whether we are acting right under all the circumstances? Or all the people connected to us by any relation or social reason are treated properly by us? Is this possible to be right always towards every single person we come in contact and everything we do? Can we take the guaranty that the circumstances do not affect our decision? I feel it's not possible. The complexity of circumstances mostly creates such situations that to decide the wrong and right becomes impossible. Hence one has to opt for the move best possible at that particular movement. If you make a wrong decision you end up being miserable, or act opposite and enjoy. Do we call it destiny or should we assume that happiness or misery is the end result of how we behave!

Further trying to relate to the circumstances of Ram's birth to find a justification of what I want to emphasize. let me tell few stories.

Ravana was blessed by lord Shiva (Mahesh) that no deva, rakshasas, animals, or gandharvas will be able to kill him. He himself was very confident that humans were no match for him. He could perish them single handed. This made Ravana over confident cruel, and reckless. He started troubling the beings of the universe and imposing himself to be worshiped by people in the world as God himself. His reckless and cruel behavior forced devas, sadhus, animals, humans and Mother Earth all to request lord Vishnu to find some solution to his atrocities. As a result Lord Vishnu decided to take birth as King Dashrath's son. Lord Vishnu had once made fun of Narad Muni creating an illusionary family for him and had later destroyed this illusion so that Narad comes to his senses. Narad got hurt and angry by this treatment and cursed Vishnu to suffer separation from his spouse and realize the pain of separation. So Lord Vishnu decided the right time for him had come for him to take birth and sort out the trouble. by taking care of Ravana, and at the same time pleasing Narad to respect his curse. Here I feel that this story is created with an aim to develop a sense of humbleness and humility in the minds of those who are stronger than others, to create a congenial relationship of the weaker with the stronger. So that we can live in harmony.

The story running parallel is that king Dasharath of Ayodhya had three queens but was childless. He decided to do yagna for getting children. As a result he got a boon that he will father four sons from his three queens. In due time Vishnu with his three assistants were born.

If we gets a chance to know all these stories we understand that they are very intricately woven together. For the simple reason that they are the incidences happened in the life of some people at a given time, whose lives were connected with each other. Through these stories we get to understand that even while trying to live in harmony, we create some disturbances in the life of people living at the same time in the society with us. For this unfortunate unintentional error too, we have to suffer. Vishnu had to be born for so many reasons as a human to settle all the disturbances in the society at that time and bring harmony in the world.

To me Lord Vishnu stands as a person who was full of an energy which could be of use in trying to settle all the differences among the people living at a particular time and direct them toward a better peaceful life. The persons of this nature are born and re born all the time are called incarnation of Vishnu. Similarly the energy to destroy the bad and worthless beings called Mahesh can be reincarnated. It is believed that lord Shiva (Mahesh) gave part of his energy to Hanuman who is also called son of Shiva. And in the period of Mahabharata the second son of Pandavas known as Bhim shared the energy of Lord Shiva, He was known for his tremendous strength. The forceful creativity of Lord Brahma is visible everywhere as nature.

Lord Krishna is another incarnation of Bhagvan Vishnu; he had to come to the world again this time to relieve the society from excesses of the Demon Kansa, later he also had a very important role to play in the war of Mahabharata. He is known as a wisest man of his time. Geeta is the discourse given by him to explain the third brother of Pandavas Arjun the importance of righteousness, truthfulness, and the importance of once duty to try and establish a good rule for common man.

Krishna was a reformer with a very open vision, his values were not different from Ram, to achieve what he thought right, he could stray away from ideology, and he was more practical this way. Ram could not tolerate the evil talks of people against his wife and divorced her. Krishna called himself a friend of Draupadi, and stood up to help her when she was being humiliated by Duryodhana and his brothers publicly. It was a shameful affair conducted in front of all those who were considered stalwarts of then existing bharatiya society, every one kept quiet and let her get insulted and humiliated for no fault of her's. Krishna was the only one who rescued her. In the story of Mahabharata the character of Krishna comes out as a very forceful and righteous individual, he never hesitated to put his opinion in front of those who needed some advice at some particular time. For Krishna it was important that a person performs his duties at the particular time with total indifference towards the benefits he is going to get by it, He expressed it during his discourse of Geeta that doing is in your hands do not worry about the outcome or the results, because it's not for you to decide what it will be (karmanye vadhikaraste, ma faleshu kadachana). If one is able to adopt the the philosophy of doing all our karma with an indifferent attitude we end up happier in the long run.

Ram was and is considered the Ideal man of his time, but he had failed many times. His failure for the first time was when he agreed for Seeta's Agni pariksha, second time when he sent her away to forest for the same reason, simply to stop the gossip mongers, and lastly when Seeta her self-rejected his offer to come back to him after Agni pariksha when he realized that she is the mother of his sons, she opted to die instead.

Seeta became the first woman of Indian society, who raised her voice against the unjust treatment given to the women. She is still an example of being a good wife, good mother and a strong person who stands against injustice. She is an ideal for many.

Ram was more of an ideologists, he was more concerned about his image as a just king with capacity of good governance. He was conscious about his projection as a socially fit king. He wanted his subjects to think about a person with a very rational and sound character. He sacrificed his personal pleasant family life because he wanted his subjects to get the message that no one under his governance is above the rules of the than existing society. He ended up doing gross injustice to his own beloved wife. Both of them must have suffered tremendous heartaches, but he endured it. His wife Seeta suffered with him, there personal life must have been under tremendous pressure, but Ram by his decisions stood out as a very just king and was called 'Maryada Purushottam' meaning most controlled in his behavior and he was best of the man of his time. Ram is known as a God by Hindus. I am not worthy of questioning this. As my understanding has grown my opinion has changed; I feel he was an ideal human being who did a lot for his people.

Even those we consider ideal man or woman are not flawless. It the democratic religious right specifically given to Hindus, since we consider our God as so much familiar and friendly with us that we do not mind telling him also where things have gone wrong by him. We still go ahead and offer prayers to him and believe that they have accepted it and we will not come to any harm, because we tried to point our finger at their mistakes.

There are innumerable reasons for me to believe that both Ram and Krishna were ordinary humans with zeal to do as much of good as possible during their life time. They were more brave then many, to fight with Ravana, and to fight Kamsa must be appreciated as a very big task for both of them. If being intelligent and daring, brave and just are the qualities needed for leader ship they both had it. That is why as ordinary human beings, people of their time must have related them as equal to God, and later on God himself.

Gautam Buddha, and Mohan das Karam chand Gandhi were also put in the category of Mahatma by the Hindu society of their times, simply because they were able to decide to do right things at right time, and to make correct decisions and stood by their conviction fearlessly under all circumstances.

Hindu religion has about thirty three million Devis (Goddesses) and Devatas (Gods). Simply because any one doing good, fighting the evil, sympathizing with the poor and those who are suffering are regarded as Godly. We do not hesitate in expressing that such person is equal to God for us. The simple reason for such attitude is that all Hindus like to believe that God is someone with a heart which can feel the pain and misery of the suffering with the same intensity of the sufferer. They want The God to live with them in their joys and sorrows, feel for them and rejoice or cry with them. when I analyze this, the God becomes a supreme emotional sensitivity of mind gifted to many of us. Thus giving the concept of thirty three million of more Gods for us,

I must say that though the concept of how we should establish a relationship with God is debatable to my mind. I have always felt that there is a supreme power which guides us all, in whatever we do. It is a force which keeps our conscious alive, which does not allow us to stray away from the truth and indulge in wrong doing or being deceitful. To me a sense of right behavior and conduct imbibed in once character is a road to religion.

4

If I was born in a Muslim family, I would have recognized myself as Muslim. For me every ritual and everything related to Allah would have been most sacred. It did not happen.

If I was born in a Christian family, I would be recognized as a Christian and would be taught all the Christian methods to worship God, recognized as Christ and going to church would have been the most beautiful thing to do. It did not happen.

If I was born in the Sikh family Gurudwara would have been my ultimate goal when I wanted to feel close to God and seek peace. It did not happen.

I was not a Jain or Jew for the same reason and so it was not possible for me to find peace at those places of worship.

The fact remains that I was born in a Hindu family. I learnt to worship God, the way my ancestors did and learnt ways and methods to behave like one.

As I grew up and developed my own ideas of how I wanted to live and be recognized, I found that I wanted to be someone who could understand myself properly and could feel comfortable in the company of others by understanding them properly. This was a very difficult task. Every one carried their religion on their sleeves and each individual thought that religion wise his/her ways were best to be adapted

There was a comment on the Facebook which said that non-Muslims are not allowed in Makka, Hindus are not allowed in the temple of Shabrimala, and there are Jews places of worship where non-Jews are not allowed. There are some temples where women are not allowed. There is Gurudwara. Place where all are allowed irrespective of their cast, religion and sex. I would like a public opinion now that if we want to feel close to God and peaceful where we will like to go. Do we really need to go to the extent of making our minds a prisoner of our own restricted ideas which love to label us as a particular religious culture and propagate them? One can neither find pleasure nor peace under such circumstances, nor God can be found anywhere around such places where humans are exposed to insults and humiliations constantly.

There is a story about a poor woman who wanted to have darshan of lord Krishna. So one day she went to the temple in the morning. The priest knew her as a poor woman of lower strata of society. He did not want her anywhere near the temple, so he discouraged her and humiliated her by saying that she had nothing to offer to the God. Therefore she was not welcome in the temple. The poor woman went back to her home and thought what she could offer God so that she will be able to see him. In her desperation she decided that whatever she does, that is all her karma, she will offer to him and ask for his darshan. Early morning when she cleaned her house and threw her garbage out she folded her hands, remember Krishna and said 'Krishnarpan' (given to God with respect). The priest when opened the door of the temple for worship found garbage on Krishna's lap. He could not think how the garbage reached there, any way he cleaned up everything and worshiped. The next day again the same thing happened. This kept on repeating for quite some time. The priest started investigation and found out that the woman was responsible for these incidences. He also realized his fault in refusing the woman for darshan (presenting oneself in front of God) he apologized to her and invited her to fulfill her wish.

The story might have been an imagination but it makes one thing clear that if we believe that there is God for us, than he is there for all.

There is another story about yet another woman who used to supply milk in one village. For this she had to cross the river which flowed between her village and the village where she supplied milk. Once it rained heavily, the river was flooded, water was flowing dangerously. She was worried, that if she did not supply milk, many children will starve. The thought was painfully troubling her, so she asked the priest who was the wise man of her village to guide her. The priest didn't think seriously about the problem and said, if you are so keen to do something, nothing can stop you from doing it. The woman took it to be the best advice. She picked up her milk pot, put it on her head prayed to God to help her and walked on the river? She distributed the milk in the village and came back the same way. The priest, who had advised her, saw her walking on the river was very surprised. He asked how she did this impossible task of walking on the overflowing river. The woman said simply, that she worked on his advice only and was very obliged by him for that. The priest was stunned. He fell on her feet and admitted that though he has advised her she turned out to be closer to God in her understanding.

This story makes me feel that God lives in our hearts and minds and make us do things which appear impossible but necessary to us. Having faith in God is more like having faith in ourselves, for this we do not need a religion. The sun rises every morning in different parts of the world, the earth circles round the sun. This causes the whether to change and also night and day to change their time and become short or long.

the cyclical presence of spring and fall. Falling of leaves or blossom every single act of nature occurs because it is bound to happen this way.

The chirping of birds, opening of flower buds, gives a message of approaching morning happens because it has to happen this way. Whether the country or place is dominated by Hindus, Muslims, Christian, or Jews or any other religion. When we claim that through our religion we can establish a relationship with God, should we not think seriously whether we need a religion for establishing our relationship with God or can we do so by ourselves with a proper frame of mind?

Poet and devotee Reydas who was contemporary to Meera bai had gone somewhere where food was being served due to some festivity. Rey das who was not an upper class and so was offered food in someone's footwear. Instead of getting annoyed Reydas laughed at the insult,and said if there is no malice in the heart even holy Ganga does not mind being put in a footwear. (Jo man changa to Kathauti (foot wear) me Ganga). Devoted humble mind of a well learned man does not need assistance of high ranking of religion. One becomes humble and full of humility, if he understands the human mind properly. To stand out with our own beliefs and stick to what we think is right is only possible if we become confident of own abilities.

Few years back there was some communal riots in U. P. (India). Some body amputated a caw's tail and left her groaning with pain on the streets. God only knows what was the religion of the person or persons who performed this atrocity on a poor animal who can't even express pain properly. I wonder if any Hindu will feel proud if he/she knew the person was a Hindu and did this heinous job to settle scores with their Muslim brothers or if the Muslim will rejoice in the knowledge that the person was a Muslim and feel happy to teach Hindus a good lesson. The main question still remains, that what do we expect by following a particular religion? Do we expect a life style which is very superior to all others who follow a different religion? Or, we want to prove that we are more closure to the God and have much better understanding about Him then people of other religions? Or, to go a step ahead we want to say that we are the best about our faith and so we should force all the other human beings to follow what we think is correct?

Probably long time ago people of different places thought and discussed as to what should be a good way to bring around all the people of a particular group under a single umbrella of socialism, so that there will be a good harmony amongst all and everyone will be happy. To achieve this goal they developed a common ground to promote the supreme power about which everyone talked differently. People of similar understanding became followers of same belief joined hands and declared their faith as a religion and thus gave birth to a philosophy to suit them. When many such philosophies were born, everybody started thinking their religious beliefs are the best and forcing others to follow them. The initial reaction to this type of clashing of ideas may not have been so bad but gradually it became a main cause to fight and prove oneself better than others. Involvement of egos and complexes created more rifts and fighting, instead of binding the humans together separation became the option. To me it appears that religions became the worse politics ever invented by humans in the name of God

We have the proof of what one religion can do to the other, when we see whatever is going on in the world for the last thousands of years or so. destruction and violence has become the way to survive. Those who think they can control the world are leaving no means fair or unfair to achieve their goal of creating turmoil. One feels sad and disgusted by this. All the places which are supposed to house God have become places of mischief crafting.

5

If we look at the history of our country, it will become very clear to us that what and who is responsible for sowing the seeds of this communal disharmony in our joint society of Hindus and Muslims.

Original Indians followed a religious culture dominated by Shevites (worshiper of lord Shiva) and worshipers of Lord Vishnu (the Vaishnavs). There were many differences amongst them about who is more superior which remained unsolved for long and were damaging to Hindu culture on the whole. When moguls invaded India they came with their own religion Islam, with the efforts of Muslims who were trying to spread Islam world over, it became necessary for Hindus to do some quick thinking to unite Shevites and Vaishnavas in theirs diversities and protect their own culture and religious believes. This emergency of religious crisis gave birth to poets and devotees like Tulasidas,Meera bai,Soordas ect. They wrote and sang the songs glorifying Shiva and Vishnu. At the same time they made the stories where both Lord Shiva and Lord Vishnu kept praising and praying to each other. Trick worked, from north to south and from east to west India became united in its religious culture and believes. The maha kavya (great book of poetry) by Tulasidas, "Ramayana" was the most successful writing.

When Soordas sang his songs about Lord Krishna's child hood and his mother's love and devotion for him, his Childhood play and naughtiness, people loved them. He created such a lively picture of the child Krishna, arguing with his mother, crying because she was punishing him. Some times when Krishna tried to play tricks on his mother and his mother Yashoda knowing fully well that her son is trying to be mischievous simply went along the whole exercise and enjoyed. The whole dramatic poetry was so fascinating, the people started seeing childhood of Krishna in every child.

When Meera bai sang and danced with devotion about her love of Lord Krishna, she created magical atmosphere around. The imaginations of common people got ignited. They enjoyed with the God his romanticism and felt very close to him. Since he was playing a very authentic human being, who was very much like them. Meera's devotion to Lord Krishna was of a different kind. She treated him as a friend and lover. With complete humility she surrendered herself to his authority. In her songs she expressed that she will do anything to be near her lover God, she sang that she will clean Krishna's place, cook for him, dress up the way he wants to see her, may be as a princess or may as his devotee. She just wanted to be for Krishna and be with him.

Again the imagination of people was charged by her devotional songs, they were going crazy by her singing and dancing, thinking of a very unique sensitive and emotional God.

During this period Tulasidas wrote the great poetic script Ramanaya. In this book of poetry which is one of the greatest literary books of its time,LordRam was personified as God presenting himself as an ordinary human being. Playing with his father, wearing ornaments suiting to the children of his age and time. crying for the moon. His father with a heart chocking with love and amusement trying to pacify Ram and his brothers. All the lovely incidents happening in the family of ordinary people were portrayed by Tulasidas in Ram and his brothers. He also took care to make disciples' of different sects of Hinduism come together by his writings and vocational expertise in the local language of the place. By reading Ramayana the public had full satisfaction of having their God as a common household member.

In Lord Krishna, and Lord Ram, Hindus got the God, they could love, play, eat, sleep, and be with. The feeling was and still is amazingly pleasant and peaceful. When one has God to give you company all the twenty four hours of your life, you don't need anybody else to worry about you. This philosophy ingrained into the minds of Hindus helped them through all the rough weather they faced during mogul invasion of India. It was not easy for anyone to shake off their faith with which they lived and breathed.

Kabir also belonged to the same era. He was a philosopher poet who had a very clear vision about religion and religiosity, God and Godism. the satirical use of language used at that time and to make a common man understand what he wanted to say was child's play to him. He made fun of Hindu orthodoxy and Muslim's excesses easily and was able to show people of his time the political use of religion by high class society preachers and priests. I would like to quote few of his pieces admired and remembered.

Kankar Panther jod ke, masjid li banay

Tape mullah bang de, Kya Bahera hua Khuday. Written to mock Muslim way of worship.

The meaning (collected the stones and rocks and made the mosque. The Muslim priest then stands on the top of it and calls loudly Allah Allah. Does he think God to be deaf?)

And to mock Hindus he sang, Pahan pooje Hari mile, to Mai poojun pahar.

Tate ye chaki bhali, pees khay samsara.

Meaning (If by worshiping stone one can meet God, then I will worship the mountains. But I think a manual grinder of stone is more worthy of worship due to its utility.)

He was crude to the extent of hurting people if they did not understand his thoughts and philosophy, and he sang aloud,

Kabira Khada bazaar me, sabki mange khair.

Na kahu se dosati, na kahu se bair.

And Kabira Khada bazaar me,liye lukathi hath.

Jo ghar phode aapna chale hamare sath.

Meaning, (Kabira is standing in the market place asking For Gods mercy for every one because he does not have enemy's or friends)

And (Kabira is standing in the marketplace, He has his stick in his hand, anyone who wants to break his family is most welcome to join him)

People understood his sentiments, loved him, respected him and followed him. He played an important role in bridging the gap between Hindus and Muslims.

Kabir understood the poison of politics spoiling the faith of people. He made them see the orthodoxy of Islam and Hinduism. He tried to make people understand the difference between being a believer and a fanatic. He produced a satirical version of religion in his poetry and was loved for it.

During moguls rule, many restrictions were put on Hindu population. They were taxed for being Hindus. The time was bad for them. Many of them succumbed to the pressure and converted to Islam, also there must have been other reasons for conversion, which forced people to become Muslims.

But India and its religion was difficult to perish. The main reason for this was that Hinduism is not only a religion; it's a way of life. Also Hindus have always been very tolerant on the whole. It also gave birth to new culture which was more acceptable for both. By new culture I do not mean new religion, but it was a way of life which made people adjust to each other's ways of life and live peacefully in harmony.

India was becoming a land of opportunity world over during sixteen to early nineteen century. Some even called it 'golden bird,' there were constant visitors from Middle East, and Eurasia, Britain was not legging behind. East India company landed in Calcutta. Portguees in the south of India in Goa,Daman. They brought Christianity, as religion, and English and French as languages and new culture. North India was dominated by the mixed race a product of Aryans and local tribes of the land. Whereas the South of India was mostly the tribes who were original Indians. These people were probably poor and ignorant, the Eurasians who brought Christianity as a religion to this part were very well accepted, because they didn't resort to violence, but helped people to overcome their poverty, become educated and live respectfully. People coming from Muslim world were also doing business in south India. They liked the land and settled there. The tribal natives of India found them very disciplined and helpful. They were attracted by these people from outside world and adapted their culture and religion. Thus India became a country of mixed culture and religion.

There were many churches built all over the country. Many mosques were also built. Christians acquired the land by taking permission from the rulers of their time. Even Muslims took permission from the rulers to build their place of worship. Unfortunately there were some mogul rulers who were more fond of implementing their views concerning religion in a dictatorial way. Their view was that the Hindu population of the country was way behind in their thinking and was wrong in the way they worshipped their God. They called those people Kaffirs who kept the statues of God in the temples and worshipped. According to them kaffirs had to be taught proper lessons, by destroying the temples, loot them and make mosques as replacement. God did not interfere in these activities of his different followers. The result was Babari Maszid and the likes. Hindus were suppressed and succumbed to the pressure of Muslim rulers of their time, but to completely wipe out the faith which was so deeply ingrained in their psyche was impossible.

At the time when Aurangzeb became the king of mogul empire. The people of Punjab were getting very upset due to the harsh treatment of the emperor given to Hindus. Panjab was always known for its bravery. Under the guardian ship of Guru Nanak (a saint) a sect was started. The followers called it Sikhism which gained prominence. It gained more popularity gradually. After Guru Nanak ji there were nine more gurus. The tenth and the last one was Guru Govind Singh. The preaching of Sikh ism is supposed to be inspirational thoughts for the good of the community. All the ten gurus added their thoughts and ideas to the book and the book is named "Guru Granth Sahib." Guru Govind Singh was the last one to add his observations and inspirations to it. He felt that to fight the moguls they have to have the army of people who are not afraid of any body and can claim to belong to a religious group who can fight for their rights like lions. He made his followers adapt a way to live and dress up in such a style they that they can be recognized anywhere without fail. Thus people belonging to this sect were called Sikhs and directed to never shave or cut their hair, carry a Kirpan (a type of weapon) with them, always put a steel bracelet on their wrist and wear a pant (kachcha) and carry a kangha (comb) These people were called Sikhs and a new religion came into practice. The Sikh religion had no casts and in this religion. Poor or rich, man or woman all were equal. They have a different concept of God. Sikhs believe that there is no place in the world where God is not present. They see him in smallest to largest creation of nature. They admire his presence in every thing happening around. They consider him as an omnipresent multi potent phenomenal. They believe in charity which is of high dimension. Feed the hungry, clothe the needy, serve the sick and do not beg. With passage of time and necessity many Sikhs have become business men, this could be regarded a zone with very thin line of rights and wrongs, but still on the whole Sikhs are regarded as good and kindhearted people. Moguls tried very hard to perish Sikhism but could not succeed, Sikhs established their own ideology and practiced it with enthusiasm. They made their places of worship in many parts of India, there were many people who appreciated the concept and followed. They created their own place in Hindu society.

Jainism and Buddhism are also the parts of sects which were born of the need of people with desire for better and more advanced thinking parts of Hinduism which was a Traditional Santana dharma.

The pure intention of this religious analysis from me is only one. That is to think and consider that we as human beings have all the time been searching an Ideology with which we try and identify our closeness to that Supreme force we call God.

The Britishers came to India, projecting the very innocent purpose to do business. No body suspected any ulterior motives of their trying to get a piece of land and set up their company. It turned out to be a nightmare of around two hundred years before India could get rid of their hold on people of India. Britishers were not happy to leave India they had enjoyed ruling for such a long time. They settled the scores by leaving the country Brocken up in two parts, of course by indulging the selfishness and egos of some of the leaders who were equally good at pleasing them. We suffered partition, with partition we suffered breaking the heart and souls of people who had lived so long in to togetherness and struggled to get their freedom together. We had a divided country on the basis of religion; on both sides we had people who lost their materialistic assets, their emotional bindings their families. And the places they were familiar with.

The country faced the biggest holocaust in the world and the largest exchange of population ever known. India became a democratic republic, but was a tragically broken nation where death and destruction was seen everywhere. Though some people sang the songs that India got its freedom without shedding blood and without fighting any war the truth was very different.

All this happened due to promoting and fanning religious differences by people like Mr. Mohd Ali Jinnah, Shri Jawaharlal Nehru. And Britishers supporting them plus Gandhi feeling helpless. No one saw any miracle happening to save the misfortune common men, women, and children were facing due to various groups of different religions without the interference of the God from any side. Only those who saw this tragedy can feel what actually happened and the disgusting sense of helplessness they were exposed to.

Wish few of the prominent and powerful personalities responsible for this calamity of partition on religious grounds had listened to their Godly voices residing in their minds and hearts. Or could it be possible that God does not live in the minds and hearts of selfish and self-centered people.

We have still not recovered from the ill effects of an untimely and cruelly devised way of partition of India.

This so called religion based atrocities gave so many opportunities to those who did not go beyond masochistic pleasures in life, to kill, curse and trample human values. God could not do anything to stop these disgusting happenings on both sides of Indian continent. Where the Muslims were in majority they were unjust to Hindus and Hindus did the same. The dance of inhumane continued and many who had accepted the ways of peaceful existence with each other's religious believes reversed back to mistrust and misbehavior towards each other, thanks to our political enthusiasts and the calculating governors of the past, the once happy and peaceful people of both the butchered parts of once a lovely country started a hateful relationship with their counterparts. The religions, which are supposed to be guide to come closure to God, became instrumental in severing the humanity. God was still quiet and watching the dance macabre.

We as most intelligent members of animal kingdom, invented religion to live in harmony with each other. It did not last long with the aim to outdo each other from various groups many religions were invented. God was classified and named differently, each group insisted that his way to address God was better than other and fights started. We became the worst type of animals who destroyed each other, killed and looted each other and insisted that our method to reach Him are the best and should be followed by one and all. It was made into a do or die rule. Ancient cultures were lost, new civilizations were established. God must have silently witnessed all.

I was a child at time when partition took place. To get actual grip on the happenings was not possible for me, but certain memories from the past still haunt me.

One is of the communal riots in our city. Just after partition, my grandmother had gone for shopping, she came back in a very panicky state and earlier than expected. Incidentally the boy next door was in our house, talking to my father, he was from the Muslim family living in the neighbourhood. When she saw him she appeared more agitated. Almost screaming with fear she told him to run back to his parents and tell them to take precaution and move fast from their house, because the rioting crowd was moving towards our street, they are in an angry mood and are targeting to crush and kill Muslims. Ikbal laughed and tried to calm her down but she kept forcing him to take early precaution. In the meantime all of us also heard the shouting of the crowd. Ikbal rushed towards his home. My father my grandmother and many others from our neighbors came out on the street. Many of them rushed towards Ikbals house. They lived on the first floor. Some of the elderly ladies went and sat on the stairs leading to their house. Some of the young man went inside the house to help them hide fast. In a very short time the agitated crowd was on our street shouting slogans and abuses against Muslims. The man folk who were blocking the staircase were trying to stop them, which was difficult. There was some punching and pushing, the goons succeeded to break the first line of defense.

Now there were women sitting on the staircase to stop them, they were all middle age or old ladies who were known to many of the people in the crowed so there was hesitation in any attempt to physically harm them; this was lucky for Ikbal and family.

The men who had gone inside the house shifted the whole family to the neighbors where they were hidden. Just then someone shouted that he saw the boy of the family jumping in the back lane which was used for the garbage collectors to collect the garbage and clean the toilets. The whole crowed ran towards the back and the victim's family got more time for rescue. From immediate neighbors they were quickly shifted to some other better and safer place. Thank God there was no killing or mishandling any one due to quick thinking of the neighbors. The next step of the goons was to loot and damage their house. It was a very bad and sickly seen. The ugliest action of humanity I and many others witnessed. When I think about I still feel a deep hurt and feel ashamed at the cruelties expressed by the human being towards other and similar humans because they belonged to a different faith.

There was constant flow of refugees from Pakistan. Almost all were Hindus running out from there for the fear of life and for the sake of the safety of their families. Many of them did not have the time and opportunity to collect some of their possessions; they had to leave in hurry to move to safer places. Just like our neighbor Ikbal's family. Many of them were shifted to the refugee camps, many lost their kith and kin. Many had their loved once murdered in front of them with cruelty. Rape murder and looting was no longer the crimes against humanity. They were day to day affairs. A refugee camp was sat close to our town. My aunt was a doctor in the civil hospital; she was put on duty in the camp for health checkup and advice. She had to go there twice or thrice in the week, once she took me to the camp as I must have been on holiday. When we were there I saw a train arrive at the station. The train was carrying refugees, I saw that it was so full that people we're overcrowding they were dangling on the compartment 's door, sitting on the windows and even on the roof of the compartments. There was no place which could be considered empty. A heart breaking cry was heard when the train stopped. I saw a woman beating her chest and crying bitterly. She was in so much pain that nothing could console her. Only God knew what she had suffered and what she had lost, but her pain was unbearable. I do not know how she was treated or whether she recovered from her trauma or not, but I still think about her and that makes me immensely sad. What was her crime? Was it enough to punish a human being because he or she belongs to a different religion? Does God whom we worship all the time, feel good and happy that we, who consider ourselves the best of all he has created so far, behave like demons towards each other just because of any religion which doesn't match our fancy.

I have lived with this nagging thought for years, have had changing ideas about how to treated religions and how to come to a compromising situation in my mind about how to adjust with people of different faiths.

Whatever is the opinion of people in general about religion and God should not matter much, as long as we understand that we may belong to different religions, but our basic reasonings are similar concerning humanity. We should respect the feelings of our fellow beings irrespective of their belief and way of life. God will always remain a guiding force in the life of majority in human community, their method of recognizing Him maybe different. Creating a discrepancy and disturbing the peace is not taking us forward in anyway.

6

It is easy to divide the human population of the planet earth into two categories. Believers who believe in God and Nonbelievers who do not believe in God. So simple and possible theoretically. When we start thinking about a unique force who is doing things for which no convincing explanation is possible, we can't think of anything else but to accept that there is universal force which is constantly working in our and every once life around us to maintain harmony in nature.

Simplest and every day happenings in our lives which have become so common are, sprouting of any seed which lay quiet for long periods without showing any sign of life, and then that seed grows into a full grown tree and produces flowers and fruits belonging to a specific species. Birth of a child of any animal is again a wonderful phenomenon. How precise the force of nature is about the process of development. We know a lot to say what will happen during a particular period of embryonic life of a particular species, but the unseen hand of the guiding force makes one believe in God who handles everything so well. We can give an explanation that why so many animals do not carry their offspring in their womb but lay eggs then nurture them by providing atmosphere for proper incubation. We can answer why this happens but then who guides these innocent creatures to prepare for forthcoming event of procreation and be ready!

If you had a chance to watch healing of wounds. I am sure every one of us had this opportunity not once but many times. The process of healing starts the moment one gets hurt. It's amazing to see how gradual and perfect the process is. Again we can describe the process in steps, help it by keeping the wound clean, but what exactly is the force which takes the control in its hands and guides the body to go in a regular progressive speed to heal with so much precision, that sometimes it is hard to find even the telltale signs of injuries. We could say its nature, but the question remains that who guides nature?

We can answer so many whys, so many how's, so many what's, but we may get stuck when we try to answer "Who!" The existence of someone watching us all the time. and is regulating all our moves and activities whether we like it or not, is a very secure feeling but at times very scary too. Scary because that Someone has provided us with a mind which can think, most of the times we like to think that we should be independent, in any and everything we do and think and express. He/She does not give us that freedom. Because freedom for all in everything they think, do or express is a way to create disturbances which can become greater disasters difficult to control. We are provided with general and special senses to protect and enjoy life. Whosoever has done this has done a tremendous favor to us.

I think about this miraculous facility to feel, touch and decide whether The thing I came in contact is useful and pleasant or should be regarded as useless and unfavorable. This makes me feel wonder struck. Makes me realize the presence of the "Who" I am looking forward to get acquainted with. It always amazes me that the same sensation of touch can arise so many different emotions; the description is not so easy. If the same person touches you at different times, and in different state of mind, the reaction and response differs. One can always make out by touch that whether it is affection, anger, lust or any other feeling the person is trying to convey. The nerve endings responding to the sensation are the same, the stimulus carried to the area of brain is also the same, but the analysis and interpretation of the feeling and emotion is different. How and why such a fine analysis takes place? Who directs it and who controls it are the final unanswered questions which point towards an answer leads us to the hands of the manipulator I would call God.

I have seen new born babies responding to their mother's touch. There is so much security and satisfaction on the face of the baby at that moment it gives tightness in my chest, and moisture in my eyes. The emotions conveyed by a simple hug or touch make me spellbound. My mind immediately starts the speculation about "Who" is making our body and mind to react to a simple action of touch, to give a flowing emotion an entirely different face every time. The answer is obvious but the mind does not get satisfied, ultimately the imagination takes over, the figures which appear to take shape as an answer are not blanks or vacuums but the Gods l have learnt from the childhood to recognize through the religious preachings, He can be a Hindu God or Christ or anyone other than these but He appears to give the answer to my "Who" and I am at peace.

Coming to special senses, again it's a miracle we are so used to experiencing on a regular basis in almost every moment of our lives that we fail to recognize them as miracles, we take them for granted. But just think, is it not amazing to have a camera fitted in our body, which is in straight contact with our brain? Curtsy this camera we can appreciate so many beautiful things and learn to avoid so many things we do not find pleasing. Similarly a fine melody or a pleasant voice could be so peaceful and soothing to us due to our hearing organ, sense of smell and taste are equally important for our exisistance and enjoyment also for safety. I feel so amazed when my taste buds tell me the difference in different eatables. We can talk about these all coming in to existence through a process of evolution, ok I am in full agreement, but only want to know "Who" manipulated this. We might come out and mention different circumstances leading to different changes in the body and then there will be many nodding their heads in agreement, but in my mind the "Who" always springs up as an unsolved mystery

I get amazed about billions of humans living in the world and each one having an individual identity in spite of having many similar looks features and even habits. We can say its natures wonder but again who guided nature to create this wonder. "Who?" There are so many small and big miraculous things happening around us all the time and we get so used to them that we fail to take notice of whatever has happened and has changed in a miraculous way. Personally I think it's the presence of the force which is omnipresent, awake, and is constantly creating, changing and modeling the activities of nature and the inhabitants of the universe for better adjustment. This force is glimpses of "The God "to me. I can feel his presence in everything and everywhere, this feeling gives me extremes of security and strength and peace to face good or bad boldly.

Very often I think of the "me" in my body and try to identify it. Believe me it's not easy. This "me" lives in my mind (should I call it brain) , in my heart (really!) And in every organ and every cell of my body. It helps to make me conscious of my being alive, in the morning when the sun rises, I become aware of its beauty. I become aware of the beauty of nature, the flowers, the vegetation around, the presence of colorful creatures surrounding me, all this gives me a feeling that

I am not alone and the feeling is very pleasant and peaceful. To become conscious of change of season, the blowing hot or cold wind the pleasant or miserable feeling of changes of season.

Meeting someone who appears very familiar and dear after becoming acquainted only for a short time. Or knowing someone all your life and still feeling him/her like a stranger not known at all. All these and much more emotional thoughts and feelings are recognized and appreciated by us due to our conscious related directly to "me." Still to try and identity the one exclusively without the presence of the body appears impossible for us. When we think of "me" or "I" an image of an individual becomes clear and it resembles the Individual which is our own body, hence the "me" becomes the body it belongs to, as long it remains alive.

The "me" we recognize in us should be identified as someone who is a guiding force in us. Sometimes we want a specific identity of our "me." Well that identity is our consciousness our soul which is there all the time we are alive. The soul is probably the smallest part of the guiding force existing in this universe. Hindus call it"Atma."when we feel lost and lonely and want some shoulder to lean on or when feel an eternal peace and want to thank someone in whose company we get a feeling of belonging we call that Supreme power "Paramatma" If there is someone who is stronger than ourselves and is able to give us the support when we need it most. That someone becomes Godly for us. Going a step further if this individual is protector, provider and helper of the masses then he is treated as a very superior being and equal to God or is treated as a king. With passage of time, such a person is given so much praises and honors that ordinary human beings start finding answers to all their with his or her help. In due course miracles are added to his or her actions and Lo! And behold! We get a God. Or we created a God. Believe me such deductions are simple and they do take place. Anywhere and everywhere in this universe.

What does the term alive means? Is it being able to eat, drink, and move around, to be able to express, procreate, to fight and show that we are powerful or to hide in the back somewhere and wait for a chance to show the world what we really are? All these appear very ordinary queries to answer, but when we think about what is going on worldwide, it needs proper evaluation. As human beings we consider ourselves to be the most intelligent animals. Unfortunately we have overestimated our intelligence, more so we are bent on proving that one race or group is more brainy then the other, we have invented various ways to separate us from each other,i.e. race, color, languages, religion, and sex. These factors not only divide us, but they also act as weapons to prove our superiority on each other. According to our race, color, languages and financial status we also claim our superiority over others and claim the rights to rule. I wonder under the circumstances that does it mean that to prove that we are alive; we should resort to all the destructive techniques? Does it mean that only when we emphasize our existence by bullying our fraternity we can claim to be alive? Do we have to emphasize our superiority over others to prove that we are alive?

When I was in school boardinghouse, I and my friend used to be eternally hungry. We used to get breakfast, lunch, evening tea and dinner. These four meals always appeared to be insufficient

Those were the days, when we got something nice and appealing to our taste we felt happy and alive. At that particular time it was difficult to understand the feeling of satisfactions giving rise to a feeling of pleasure which lead to a sense that you are alive. Sometimes simple things in life make you so happy, so alive. As a child eating was a pleasure having and doing certain things one finds happiness in was also great pleasure... feeling lively or alive?

Scientifically being alive could be a different story, but if we are human beings in reality, then to be alive means to live with some values which make you feel proud of what you are and what you want to be.

To give authenticity to this experience, there are few incidences I would like to share.

In my family my mother used to get seasonal fruits regularly. It was her belief that fruits eaten regularly can help in maintaining immunity. It was a rule that after dinner we all had fruits regularly. In winter a huge basket of oranges was purchased. It was kept in the store room. She used to bring out oranges by numbers to be distributed to us on a big tray. On that particular day one orange was less in the tray. Ma was sure that one of us kids had taken it. She was very particular about everyone getting his or her share and suspected that one of us four had taken away one piece without telling her, this was a very bad behavior amounting to stealing. So the inquiry started. both of my brothers my sister and I were interrogated no body confessed. Then she hit upon an idea, she said.

One of you has eaten the orange without asking me, if the person confesses to doing it, I won't be angry but I will feel happy that you have the guts to confess your mistake. Otherwise I can't help but punish all four of you. In case no body confesses I will have to stop buying fruits because to me your character has to be stronger, that is my first priority. If you, whoever has stolen the orange confesses, not only I will be happy for you confessing your guilt. I will also give one additional orange to the person speaking the truth.'

I felt that it was a tricky situation, I did not know who had stolen the orange, but I could guess that my mother is upset that one of us had done it. If no one comes forward then we all will be the suffering. If Supposing I confess then not only I get the extra orange, it will also make her happy. I could not analyze the hows and whys of the situation but decided to take the blame on me. I did it get an extra orange, and everyone was relieved. I did not know anything about the lost orange, but I could bring a situation under control and was happy about it.

The whole idea to remember this story today is the experience I got from the incident. Whatever was my intention I was successful in bringing peace to my mother's mind and was benefited by an orange. Talking of this incidence with reference to the conscious, I feel that if by not harming anyone our being slightly tactful brings harmony and happiness it's worth it. But we should know our limits and not make it a habit. Another thing conscious is present in all minds, we have to keep it alive, and be lively. Awaken the guiding force existing in our selves is a good way of being close to the one who is responsible for us.

———————◆———————

7

Religion for every one is a very sensitive issue. We are very proud of the religion we belong to. We are very protective about the religion we follow, we also feel very happy if we hear someone talking something good about our religion. Whether we have proper knowledge of our religion is a thing we do not want to share with any one from our own religion or someone who is follower of some other religion.

Still at times awkward moment arise when something happens and we get to see the face of ours or someone else's from other religion. I had my basic education in Christian schools. It was a time when India was only a few years old after independence. It was a routine that Bible was discussed in the moral science period. I do not remember having objection to this, or any of my classmates having any problem about it. But one fine day one of us heard somebody saying that now since we have become independent, we need not study Bible. All of a sudden a wave of retaliation started. Everybody in the school started talking about it. Then one day all the Hindu girls declared that we refuse to study Bible. Since we are Hindus we should not be forced to study Bible nor will we give any test for it.

I personally did not realize the seriousness of the matter, the head mistress of the middle school section was deeply disturbed. There was a meeting of school board, and ultimately they decided to withdraw Bible teaching from moral science. We still talked about what was ideal behaviour. Importance of truth in life, and how we should save ourselves from being deceptive. No one in the school talked about this incident, the transition from Bible teaching to the teaching about morality was subtle and non-disturbing. As far I was concerned studying about Christianity was not very bad, the girls retaliated against is because somebody wanted them to do it. Majority of our teachers were Christians but even from them there was no reaction of anger or dislike towards any Hindu girl.

Why I participated in that movement is hard to explain, the only explanation I can think of is the spirit of mass movement dragged me. This is a very common phenomenon. The enthusiasm of the masses makes us do something we cannot expect we are capable of. I regret participating in that exercise.

There were many workers in my school working in various capacities, I did not think about them the way I do now. Like their names. There were few teachers, their names were I.e. Miss Sulochana Paul, Miss Lal, Miss Ram, and Miss Geeta Mathew etc. There were some doing lower category jobs like driver, peon, cleaner,cooks,attendants. They had names Rechal Rajaram Kisandas James,Sangeeta Francis,Moti cook,Jeeta John and so on, their names were significant to me because they suggested the Hindu origin of these people, who must have converted to Christianity due to whatever reasons. Whether they were forced off did this out of some need is also not known to me. I only know that when Christians came to India in search of better postures. There were some people in India who embraced Christianity to suit their need and circumstances.

There are certain circumstances which need to be considered while thinking about the people of different religions trying to convert to some other. Poverty, bad treatment by people of same religion due to someone belonging to a low cast or lower strata of society. Every person alive in this world has a right to preserve his/her own dignity and self-respect. This has been one of the worst drawback of Hinduism that we have created a class in our group who are kept on very high pedestrian, and the other at a very low level. The two different strata cause so much conflicts that those who have to keep feeling that they have been denied the feeling of having any self-respect, have to search the means to keep it intact by any means available and conversion is the convenient one. If people of other religious conviction are ready to accept these people who are looked down upon for no reason or fault of theirs and so have decided to convert, to me it appears justified.

There are very few evidences against Christians that they forcibly tried to convert anybody to Christianity. There are incidences where they told the poor and neglected tribal in India and Africa that if they convert or accept Christianity, they will benefit. On the other hand this is also true that somewhere along the line western world has been color conscious and have treated coloured people as lesser humans. Thus have stood almost similar to the Hindus in their castism. With development of understanding and international integration of people from all society these issues of color prejudice and cast definitely have reduced a lot but, have not disappeared completely.

In India from the time unknown the cast system has been criticized, but has persisted. Just closure to the time when India was about to achieve independence, there was a man who came from a lower cast back ground. He was called Bhimrao Sapkal later he was given the sir name Ambedkar by one of his teachers after the name of the village he belonged to.

He contributed a lot for the progress of India towards independence; He was an intelligent and conscious person. He himself had suffered the atrocities of high cast people. His own humiliation had put him a position where it was essential for him to think of a way of saving others and himself from this ugly behavior of upper class. Education was one such way, but for getting proper educational qualifications resources were needed. The king of Baroda was an elite man. He was keen on India's progress, and the uplifting of Indian society was possible when its low cast downtrodden people were given a chance to develop and progress in right direction was his thinking.

He helped Bhimrao Ambedkar to further his education and was instrumental in sending him to U K for improving his educational qualifications. Bhimrao Ambedkar held qualification in law and was a well-qualified person. He wrote the constitution of India, and got Doctorate for it.

After completing his education when Bhimrao returned to India, India had not changed much, low cast people still suffered the humiliation for no fault of theirs, this was a situation which disturbed him He wanted a way out. When India got freedom and he was assigned the responsibility of writing down the constitution of India, which was very well done by him and he became well known for this. The thought of difficulties the Dalits (low cast people) were facing was a constant cause of suffering. Ultimatly he came to the conclusion that accepting Buddhism could be a solution. So he himself accepted Buddhism and encouraged all those who could understand his philosophy. So on 14th Oct 1956 a large number of Dalits were converted to Buddhism from Hinduism. This ceremony took place in Nagpur a city in Maharashtra at Deeksha Bhumi as it is known this was supposed to be a good solution for the downtrodden at that time.

The Dalits in India who suffered for a very long time were happy now that they had a new Identity. But this was not a hundred percent guarantee to peace and happiness. There were still many issues to be sorted out for them. To me it appears that changing of religion has only been like changing attire. The actual change will come when they also are educated and have proper understanding about their own internal problems. There appears to be a subtle undercurrent between those who have become Buddhist and Hindus. Obviously religion has not offered any substantial solution. The ideology of Buddhism is very different from what is practiced by Buddhist who has adapted Buddhism, one can feel the anger and anguish they feel for the society and religion they followed earlier. They feel more comfortable living in a community surrounded by their own group; amongst themselves they differentiate each other from each other by tracing their Dalit ancestry. This attitude clearly shows that they are still the targets of their own prejudices. The only way out of this complex situation is to understand in one's own mind the problem and then expel it out of their system. Of course for achieving this aim our society has to help, not by promoting the reservation for the schedule cast and society, but for economically lower section of the society and taking care of giving them proper education. This is the only way we can bring up every section of the society at par with each other.

I also feel that when a person is asked to submit his/her bio data for any job, the column for mentioning the cast and religion should be scrapped out. Economic status is fine if needed. When at administrative level this decision will become mandatory the common people will start following it automatically and they will give importance to their own ability for what they want to pursue as carrier. The complications one suffers due to cast and creeds will be wiped out before we realize. The only columns to recognize the individual identity should be limited to nationality and the place (address) the person belongs to. Let the individual be judged by the qualities and the qualifications he has.

This is one of the only ways to rid of politics of religion and casteism. Education and upbringing of and individual should not depend on his race, cast. Religion and colour. It should be judged on the qualities one possesses as a human being, with a live consciousness towards a fellow human being and towards a very alive nature. If we are able to give up boasting about religion publicly it will automatically become more ideal and more human, plus it will be a better admired notion with an understanding God.

The special provisions provided in our constitution to Dalits also have become an eyesore for other Indians. Any high class Indian who works hard to achieve high grades and expects to join a good professional institution to further his carrier gets an ugly kick, when he or she is rejected on the plea that a Dalit has got admission against reserve quota and he is rejected even after getting better marks. Even the selection in jobs same things like this happen and a more capable candidate is rejected against a non-deserving Dalit due to reservation quota. In general, a situation has developed where it is frustration all over. The student who gets admission against reservation quota many times does not do well because he or she is not capable. So he is frustrated, the one who gets selected in job through reservation faces the same situation and becomes a victim of mockery by his colleagues. He or she settles the scores by taking out their frustration on their juniors and other colleagues. The changing of religion does not help much but creates more difficult situation. Mixture of religion with politics to create a more complicated situation hard to handle for anyone. The only persons who get benefitted by religion are politicians. They show their pseudo sympathy to the one suffering, shed crocodile tears to ensure their vote bank, if they win in election they adopt the means to increase their bank balance, then live in luxury and enjoy life. When another election time approaches, they are again ready with similar tricks to fool ordinary simple citizens who are used to dreaming that they will have better time in near future.

The one and only solution to such a situation is better and good education to all poverty stricken population. To wipe out the notion from their minds that they will benefit by producing the proof of their being backward cast or community wise. Once it is lawfully decided that there will not be any body backward or superior by birth, a person should be considered able by proving his ability, the condition for everyone will improve for better living.

I definitely do not mean that Babasaheb Ambedkar (Bhimrao Ambedkar) was wrong to make so many to change their religion. He thought it the best way for people at that time, but for the uplifting of any society or any individual, there can't be a better option to education and exposure. To me it seems that religion card did not work so well.

Another example where religion became a curse for human beings in India was seen in 1984. After Mrs. Indira Gandhi was assassinated, there was mass anger against Sikhs. They were brutally tortured and murdered. To this day it is hard to find any justice in what happened at that time. Humanity suffered by the hands of monster souls. The thought of following any religion became a questionable way if the religion teaches brutality of this extent.

The suffering of humans during partition of India in nineteen forty-seven is vivid in my mind even today. It is beyond any bodies imagination, how brutal people turned towards their own friends and neighbors due to the other person or party having different religious faith. Humanities must have shed tears of blood at that time. To me belonging to any religion started giving a feeling of shame. To top it all God who witnessed all these criminalities, just kept quiet. If we expected any miracles to save innocent civilians, it did not happen. As a normal person if I think about all this I feel that during such periods of intense civil crisis if we cannot keep our consciousness alive in our hearts the God residing in our minds and hearts becomes stunned with shock and refuses to react, then devil takes over and religion becomes a roguish tool.

The looting, killings, and various crime committed by those who in their enthusiasm to expand their territories invaded India many times is well stated in the history. There must be some who like to sing the songs of glory about them., but whenever these chapters from the past are opened I feel extremely saddened at the attitude of such people who preferred their personal ego and misconception of their fame as the brave-hearts who crushed and killed ordinary innocent civilians to establish themselves as rulers of the land.

There are such forces alive and working even today; who think that to rule terror is the best option. If they succeed. I am sure our planet will become a miserable place to live. The God who gives us guidelines towards peaceful living will go stunned and will not perform miracle. And religions will be playing more roguish roles. In Pakistan a young boy was arrested while he was presenting himself as a suicide bomber. He was apparently brainwashed and was willing to die because whatever he thought or understood about God, he was sure he was doing right thing and had earned his place in paradise. The amusing action from his side was that he had secured his private parts with a steel sheet. because he was going to enjoy the company of jihadi girls, hoors (beauties) in heaven. So much of brainwash by people of roguish religious concepts who want to spoil the peace and happiness of ordinary simple and innocent people of the world they want to rule.

My curiosity arises when such things I read somewhere or if by chance you hear someone talking nonsense about their wish to rule the world. God belonging to which religion, wants his world to be guided, directed or disciplined in cruel ways where looting torturing assaulting and killing makes world a miserable place to live.

There was a family staying close in my neighbour, they can't be called as family friends but we knew them for long. When their son went to college, he became friendly with a girl from his class. There was nothing wrong with the girl or his family accepts that she was from a different cast. There was so much and so many problems created for this when they decided to get married. The parents of the girl said that they will break all relationships with her if she gets married to the boy of her choice, if he is not from their cast and community. The boy's parents were equally adamant, they said that if a girl from a different cast and community is accepted by them as their daughter in law, it will be very hard for them to find proper alliances for their other children in their own community.

There was so much of discussion, verbal fights and even exchange of abusive language with each other. Ultimately the boy decided to leave his parents' house and the girl did the same? They both were educated and adults who were capable of taking their own decisions. They got married in court, and settled down in their own house. Time passed, both set of parents did not reconcile with their children. Later the new family increased in number and also they did well in life. Their financial status improved and their respect in the society also was perceptibly nice. There were people in their friend circle who did not mind the difference of cast and community of married couple, the change in the outlook of many such individuals brought change in the attitude of older parents and the families were united after a long gap of few years. It was sad that on the whole they missed so many incidences they could have enjoyed together and would have so many things shared with each other. Simply because of not being able to accept a different culture of the family they were related to. Somewhere along the line their religious perceptions were wrongly interpreted by them.

Was it a wrongly under stood version of religion, a misunderstanding about culture, which is closely related to God and God ism or both, we have to decide ourselves. Such incidences are a clear sign of darker political effects of religion on the society.

8

When God becomes an issue to start a fight, like it is happening in the world today, he loses his Godliness. Then He becomes the devil we do not want to live with.

To most of us religion means a method to worship and recognize God. There can be many methods we use to worship God. This tradition of worship has been going on for a very long time and has accommodated many political views to give it different faces.

In fact the evolution of humanity is very closely related to evolution of religion.

Hindu culture and religion have stood up the test of time and changes in the thinking of humans for almost twelve thousand years. Or so. The only reason for this stability is because it is not only a religion which makes a person fearful of the anger of the Supreme power we call God, but it gives a person an understanding that his God lives with him or her all the time under all circumstances. He is a well-wisher a guide and a friend through thick and thin. Having so much faith on someone whom we have never seen and will never see is not possible for a person who likes to see and feel his or her God everywhere with him or her.

I have a friend who is a devotee of Lord Krishna. In her pooja room every single dish cooked in the kitchen has to be offered to Shrinathji. So for lunch before the food is served on the dining table Shrinathji's plate is served in pooja room. She herself takes the food there. Same happens during evening snacks period and then at dinner time. I felt very amused to witness all this, and the most amusing thing happened when I heard her talking to her cook about some vegetable which she did not approve of, she told him to be care full about such careless mistake because she does not want shrinathji to suffer in silence. While she was talking to her cook, I found that she was very sure that Shrinathji is very important member of the household. She was careful and particular about taking care of the needs of her God in a perfect way. I Found her care and devotion very interesting and touching. Not even for a small moment I felt that the way she attends to her God has any element of playful attitude or insincerity. She did something in which she had complete faith and she enjoyed whatever she was doing.

By this experience I understood what a true devotee meant when he or she says that they are inviting the God to stay with them! The poetic description of Ramayan or the expression of Meera bai's romantic version of poetry written for Krishna. I. Also understood why our people who are Hindus, religion wise are so cool and accept what fate offers them in such a dispassionate way.

As a Hindu who is in company of The God for every single moment of his life, it becomes absolutely nonessential to go to temple or spend time doing pooja. One has to understand this sentiment by going through it. There are many people who may not agree to what I am saying because this is a totally unique and absurd feeling. But at the same time they do not object to each other calling themselves belonging to Hindu religion. This is because tolerance is the basic quality a Hindu possesses. That is why we say that Hindu is not a religion, its way of life. If somebody forces a Hindu to change his way of life it's almost like killing him.

I do not believe that there is a hell and heaven created separately somewhere else. But there is a story about differentiating true love for God and an understanding him rightly. so I am inclined to share with all.

Once Narad Muni went to heaven to meet God, he found that Lord Vishnu was supervising the building of a house there. Narad was curious so he asked Vishnu the reason for personally supervising the construction, and for whom. Lord Vishnu told Narad Muni that the house was being constructed for a very profound devotee of him, who was supposed to leave the world in a few days. Nard was surprised and curious, after all who could be more devoted to the Lord more than him. Reading what was going on in Nard's mind Lord Vishnu advised him to go to the world and see for himself.

Narad came to the world and went to the place as directed by Lord Vishnu. He was a silent and un noticed observer in this case. He found that the house he wanted to keep under scrutiny belongs to an old farmer and his family. In the morning when the farmer got up just before day break, he folded his hands and remembered the God, he told God that he had a very nice and peaceful sleep so he is very thankful to Him for His kindness. Then he picked up his clothes and walked towards the pond where he had morning routine of bathing and cleaning and came back home. His wife had his food ready and served him, he quietly had his meal, then picked up his farming tools and went to his farm. The whole day he worked on his land. He met some of his friends in between and exchanged pleasantries. In the evening at sun set he collected his tools and his buffalos and came back home. By the time he washed himself clean, his wife was ready with the dinner, so he sat down for eating. After eating he and his wife had some casual talk and then he went to bed. Before falling off to sleep he folded his hands in abeyance and told God that because of His mercy he was able to do the daily routine properly and he is very thankful for the same., then he requested the God to take care of his mind and body for him, to protect him from doing anything wrong and to keep similar mercy on everyone. He closed his eyes and was fast asleep immediately. Narad Muni observed that this was the routine followed by the farm all the time for all the days. he was surprised at what did Lord Vishnu found so impressive?

He wanted an answer for his query, so when he went back to ask Lord Vishnu, what was the reason to call the farmer, his great devotee. So that Lord Himself has to supervise building the house for him? Vishnu laughed and said, oh friend didn't you notice, whatever the farmer does from morning till night he devotes it all to me with a very sincere attitude, he has never asked for anything else but to be close to me. Don't you think I can do at least this much for him? Nard was speechless at the magnanimity of both, the devotee and his God!

The story is an explanation, how a simple mind works and communicates with the God. The simple person with simple mind can belong to any religion, the beauty is that he keeps his God in his heart and derives his strength from Him. Such stories can be found circulating in all the faith all religions.

This story was very inspiring for me. Not because I believe in a separate heaven and hell but because the two persons who are described in one story. The God and His devotee have such a good understanding towards each other. They appear to me as supportive of the same thinking process, (you care for me and I care for you). It appears to me as if it is one mind doing favors for both. That is how a Hindu thinks, he cannot and will not separate himself from his God. Such a devotion is impossible to change it flows in the vessels of Hindu with his blood. For them God, Religion and him or her are one entity.

Buddhism which is a diversion from Hinduism also supports the same philosophy. Gautama Buddha believed in a society where there was no body too big in status and no one was too small. He did not preach having different rules for poor and rich. upper cast or lower cast. Buddhists do not believe in separate hell or heaven beyond this world. They believe in karma, and their opinion is that by your karma you create your own hell or heaven. He taught people to be tolerant and be sympathetic towards each other. He wanted people not to kill or hunt for fulfilling their hunger. He wanted everyone to live happily without troubling the others. To achieve a state where everyone is happy and satisfied is not possible but still whatever he taught was good to be followed and is good still.

Gautama Buddha was clever in picking the incidences happening around and using them as lessons to be taught to his disciples. His art of teaching was good and easy for learning with his followers. He was more a philosopher than a religious preacher.

Gandhi was very similar to Buddha. He also preached Ahimsa, worked against casteism, and religious discrepancies. Like Buddha he went to those who needed help and tried to relieve them of their miseries.

Buddha was going somewhere with his followers he found a very sick man lying by the side of the road, he was smeared in his own excreta and was smelling filthy. No one wanted to go near him, but Buddha sat beside him cleaned him, treated him and made him comfortable. He felt compassionate towards all who were suffering. He wanted a human society capable of loving and caring for each other. The world will become a better place to live if we all learn to love and care each other was his message to all. He wanted his message of love care and compassion to reach as many people as possible.

He wanted everyone to have high morals. And put lot of value on truthful, and sincerity of character. He was a promoter of equality to all in terms of health wealth and education. He tried to spread his ideas in the world by travelling extensively and meeting people everywhere.

There is a story about Buddha telling how he dealt with blind followers of certain customs. There was a man who lost his father, to help his father reach heaven and achieve nirvana, he thought that nobody could be better than Buddha to help him perform the rituals. so he went to Buddha and requested him to do this favor. Buddha agreed and asked him to get two earthen pots, one filled with pebbles and the other filled with butter. The man went and got the two pots as directed. Then Buddha told him to go and put both the pots in the pond in the water Thinking that it is best to do as Buddha tells him, he put the pots in water in the pond. When he came back Buddha asked him to get a strong stick and break the pots. The man who had already performed the funeral of his father was slightly surprised that why he has to this ritual again since the ceremony to break the pot after taking the parikrama of the funeral pyre is done early, but he did not question and did what he was asked to do. When the pots were broken the butter from its pot started floating in the water, whereas from the pot of pebbles, the pebbles spluttered out and got scattered at the bottom of the pond in the water. The man who was confused that what he should do now looked at Buddha for advice. Buddha smiled and asked him to push the butter down and bring the pebbles on the surface of the water. The man was highly confused and also agitated by this request from Buddha and told him that this is not possible.

Buddha then smiled and asked him to calm down and explained to him that any amount of rituals are not going to help his father to achieve going to heaven or hell. If he has been a good man all his life and has been smooth as butter he will go up to heaven otherwise if he is burdened with wrong doings and sins then he is destined to settle down in hell like pebbles in the floor of the pond. So he should go home and pray. That is all he can and should do for the departed soul.

Such a simple way to explain that you reap what you sow. That was Gautama Buddha a very religious but non-religious man.

Mahatma Gandhi as he was known among the people in India for his high moral values and his ideology was also similar to Buddha in many ways. His struggle for self-searching might have started much earlier in life, but it became noticeable during the time he worked in South Africa. When he noticed the treatment given to dark skinned and brown people by the white skinned people. He himself was victimized at times. The worst insult he faced when he was thrown out of the first class compartment of the train in South Africa because he was a colored man and he should not have dared to sit in the same compartment with white passenger. The incident is very well known and is quoted a most everywhere by all authors who have written about his life.

Gandhi realized the ill treatment imparted to Dalit people in India by their own community of Hindus, this disturbed him very much and he worked hard to improve the situation. He gave Dalit people a name Harijans, meaning people belonging to Hari (God) himself, but the trick did not work. The Dalits themselves started disliking being called by this name. As far as he himself was concerned Gandhi related the condition of Dalits due to their unhygienic ways of living and he tried hard to teach them and everyone else to learn to live in a clean way. He gave the slogan "Cleanliness is Godliness" to all Indians. He worked on teaching Indians high morals, value of truth, honesty, love and care. He changed his living style to that which was affordable to the poorest of the poor. He was called a half necked man mockingly by many of his friends.

To start with Gandhi was not a very vocal man. But his stint as a lawyer in South Africa opened him up. Also it gave him the purpose in life. He returned to India as a different person. The purpose was to make India a free country where people could live according to their thinking and lead their lives as free people who could think freely, behave freely, earn their living as they preferred and voice their opinion freely and should not feel like slave in their own homeland. He wanted to educate his people about the art of living together happily. To love, to care and understand the meaning of kindness and friendship.

Gandhi was born and brought up In a Hindu, vegetarian family, with traditional Hindu values. As he grew up in his thinking he did not leave his values behind,but found himself getting more conscious and clear about what he had learned as a child. He must have put a lot of efforts to know about other religions but that did not make him give up his religion, In fact he became more convinced that whatever his religious following was he perfectly fitted into it, but he did not become disrespectful of any other religion. His favorite prayer was "Raghupati Raghav Raja Ram, Patit pavan Seeta Ram,Ishwar Allah tere nam, Sabko sanmati de Bhagwan."

For Gandhi, religion as an instrument to create turbulence was not important, rather he wanted it to be helpful to create a bridge between the people of different faiths to understand and learn to live, love and respect each other.

There is an incident of his life which shows his eagerness about this. Gandhi was in Calcutta at the time when Hindu Muslim riots broke out, people of both the religions started fighting and killing each other, looting and harming each other became a common scene. Gandhi became upset. No one was prepared to listen and be sensible. He resorted to fasting, to tell people that this disturbs him. After few days of fasting when his health started deteriorating, everyone became worried, but Gandhi was adamant that either people of both the sects listen to him or he is prepared to die. There was worry and concern about the situation with no possible outcome. Suddenly a Hindu man from the poor background of Hindu community came to visit him, he was taken to Gandhi. The man was angry and frustrated. He took out a piece of bread from his pocket and offered it to Gandhi and asked for a solution. Gandhi told him to go home and get an orphaned Muslim child with him and raise him with care and love, with caution to teach him that the child becomes a good Muslim when he grows.

Such a fascinating solution to complex religious problem created by the political parties of the time, only a person of Gandhi's understanding could find!

It's a matter of shame for us, that we had such a good thinker from our country, but we could not understand his values of life properly! Nobody is flawless in this world. Gandhi was no exception. During his life as an active member of congress his struggle for freedom was matchless. His popularity amongst the masses was beyond imagination. I had been a witness to this once, when he crossed Bilaspur station in old CP. of India where my aunt was serving as a doctor. One of my uncles took me to the station to see him. We found it hard to enter the platform. When the train arrived all the people on the platform started shouting slogans in his praise., everyone was trying hard to get his glimpses. I was a small kid it was hard for me to see him simply by standing on my own. So my uncle picked me and put me on his shoulder.

L saw Gandhi standing on the compartment's door; He was folding his hands saying Namaste to all.

People could not stop cheering. The sight was overwhelming. A short thin and balled man looking just like any ordinary person from the street was focus of so much attention and affection. People kept cheering and chanting slogans till the train did not start moving again. He kept waving his hand till he could be seen. The sight was so enchanting that I can't forget it.

This was Gandhi who lived in the hearts of Indians as their very own family member, his simple charm glowed on his face and people believed everything he said. He was a religious man a Hindu by birth. I do not know whether he followed any routine rituals or not but he always prayed morning and evening. His prayer meetings were famous in his ashram. Yet he never made any attempt to criticize any other religion any time. He was a staunch supporter of the fact that all religions are the methods to be close to God and he told everyone to understand this and follow them according to their choice.

I feel Gandhi gave new dimensions to Hinduism.

Gandhi's vision and hope for seeing all the religions practiced in India to be together with care and love was given a setback by Jawaharlal Lal Nehru and Mohd Ali Jinnah.

Both of them were bent upon acquiring the highest office In India and were not bothered so much about keeping the nation as one. Jinnah who was never a strict follower of Islam but was against Hinduism. Though it was very well known to Muslim community of India, there was some who rejoiced about having a separate country backed by some of his supporters his ambition flared up and the result was that he started showing his preference for a Muslim nation separately and Nehru in his enthusiasm for becoming first priminister of India overlooked all the negativity the circumstances would create. Gandhi was sidelined and became alone. The beautiful country was divided into Hindustan and Pakistan, on the basis of religion. God must have cried tears of blood after that. Not only the two parts of a single country divided the people, they started hating each other.

Jainism is also a religion close to Hinduism, This religion also preaches True good behaviour, honesty, and ahimsa and respectful behaviour. Followers of Jain dharma are also believers of tolerance towards fellow beings and nonviolence. People may be following the principles of any of these sects but they have lived peacefully with each other and have been happy together.

In Jainism the main thing they insist upon is self-reliance, Jains insist on not expanding your needs more then you can afford. Self-control is the basis of success. First deserve then desires is the main Moto of Jains. The Jains are business community of India and their religious commitments are based on the better, sincere, and honest ways to earn profits and use of their wealth.

Christianity was introduced to India through Portuguese and Britishers. It was something new. The story of birth of Christ was fascinating. That he was son of God who was sent to the world, to look after the problems the people were facing and to solve them. There is talk of lots of love to our fellow beings. Doing things to help people in trouble. To help the sick and needy. There are Catholics who pray and follow different methods for praying. One can find the statue of mother Mary and Jesus Christ on the cross in every Catholic Church. There is another branch of Christians called Protestants. The Protestants do not have any idols in the place of worship.

Their churches are the places to pray and pay respect to God. whatever I Have understood about their understanding about God is that recognize to him as a source which has created the world for them to live and enjoy. God created Adam and Eve and provided them with everything for their pleasure. Every single thing in this world is for the use of human beings who are the most superior of all the living objects here. There are Ten Commandments given in the religious texts which are the instructions for disciplinary conduct of a true Christians

These are:

- I am your lord The God, I have got you out of the crisis. you will worship only me and no one else.

- You will not bow in front of any one else as God.

- You will always respect your parents

- You will not participate in murder

- You will not speak lie

- You will not speak against your neighbor.

- You will not indulge in adultery.

- You will follow Sabbath.

- You will not do idol worship

- You will love your neighbor.

Christians also feel that through religion they could rule the world. I got surprised when I read this statement while searching about Christianity as a religion. I had the impression that Christianity is about love compassion, sharing and sacrifice. You can't even rule a bird if there is no love and compassion in your heart. The feeling of love and being loved is so great that it fills the heart with so much gratitude that we start saying 'Love Is God 'There are so many stories about Christ where he healed people simply touching them. Such is the power of love that in today's world it is preached as one of the arts of healing.

The Christianity is divided into many groups like Protestants, Catholics, seventh day Adventists etc. They are believers of Christ, but they do not prefer to pray in each other's churches. It is surprising why they are so particular about not sharing their places of worship and why do they feel they are different from each other.

The basis of all the religions leads all the people towards a simple life governed by truthful behavior, honesty. Kindness and love and care. In all the religions there are stories which encourages one for good conduct and sincerity which is appreciated by God.

There is no religion in the world which teaches disrespect towards woman, but there is one religion which says that God created woman for the pleasure and entertainment of man. The people who are followers of this religion feel that they follow the best religion of the world, they feel that everyone in the world should follow whatever is preached in their religion. If they do not follow what is said in their book of preachings, then such persons or people are non-believers and they should be forced to follow what is prescribed by their religion or they should be killed and tortured and killed.

The followers of this religion can freely express their views and feelings about other religions of the world but they are extremely sensitive if they hear some comment not to their liking about their own faith. They get angry and many times violent. They does not tolerate any criticism of their religion.

The religion is called Islam and the God is called Allah. As of today Islam is the religion followed by majority of people in the world. Does this mean that Islam becomes number one ideal faith to be followed by all the people in the world without any idea of analyzing what our own feelings are and what our minds tell us to do?

I suddenly understood the intricacy of religions making their web around the force of energy whom We identified as God, without liking the idea of dividing it into so many fractions to become the guiding force to be recognized as God. The effort is to enclose everything big or small living or nonliving into an embrace. Thus giving them a sense of security that they will be looked after. Unfortunately human minds refused to see the God's hands hidden behind. If any religion and person or a group of people belonging to any particular religion think of making it a tool to rule the world. the idea itself is born as a sickness which should be treated accordingly. The religion which is followed by majority of the people is suffering from this sickness and appears to be at the brink of breaking. It has developed so many fractions inside one big body that it is become impossible for it to identify the sense from nonsense. There is fight between different broken parts to outdo each other, plus to establish their superiority over the other religions of the world there are threats and terrorizing tactics are also in use. Common and simple people the world over are confused, afraid and sad. They do not know whom to trust, the result is a broken scared and frustrated human society.

The question is who is more valuable, The God who created the universe or the religion, which created different Gods, or the God who resides in our hearts and minds and keeps guiding us all the time?

There is no reason to fear God, because he lives with us all the time to guide us an direct us towards what is right. As long as we listen to our conscious and do what is required of us. It is nature's rule you do something wrong and you are bound to suffer the consequences. Nature has no forgiveness even for the smallest mistakes we commit. For example you eat too much, you suffer from indigestion. You don't sleep properly you suffer from confusion. One has to be very careful with nature; it is very revengeful and does not loose time in settling the scores. The proof is in so many natural disasters we have to face worldwide. Nature can be regarded as our best friend if treated with respect, and worst enemy if we don't. The nature can be regarded as a most fearful face of God. We should learn to flow with the wind!

9

There is a devil existing in every mind which tries to contradict everything which the God tells it to do or follow. These two, the Devil and the God are like twin brother's. One is equally powerful as the other. Depending on the circumstances and the influences, the mind undergoes from the childhood, the ruler of the individual's personality is either Devilish or Godly. There are always rule breakers, meaning it's not essential that all those who are born and brought up in similar surroundings turn out to be opposite to each other, or just like a mirror image personalities. Somehow the rule of the nature is never to make two identical personalities. Even when they are two identical twins. They might physically look alike, they might think similar things, but when it becomes essential to map out the total personalities, there will definitely be some difference somewhere by which they can be identified. I find it miraculous and appreciate the handicraft of the God through nature.

It might have been a balancing act of nature to create good as well as bad everywhere. As human beings also same has happened, there are human beings who like to live in harmony. let us call them symbiotic by nature. They love to live in company, do various things together and enjoy life. Such people do not want trouble and on the whole are happy and satisfied benign type.

There is a second category of human beings who always want more than they have. They want everyone to listen to what they have to say, they want others to do as directed by them and if somebody does not do what is desired by these dominant types of humans, he is asking for trouble. They are the trouble makers in the society of human beings. These are the people who do not belong to any group any sect or religion. They like to have some disturbance going on somewhere in the society of human beings all the time. They survive on such activities. At a smaller scale when they are in the process of evolving into a bigger mischief monger, they commit smaller crimes to establish themselves for a bigger future in the world of crime. Once they are established, then there is no limit to their ambitions. Also there is no place where they can be restricted or not found. They are master conman, good actors, and experts in deception. There is no place in the world where such people don't exist.

We had a P.M of India, Lalbahadur Shastri, the simplest and most sincere man one could find. Before finding faults with others, he looked for his own record to justify himself. He was railways minister in Jawaharlal Nehru's cabinet. Ones there was a major accident of railways during his tenure, he felt so bad at the loss of lives of the innocent that he offered to resign. Nehru had to make him understand to not to take this step.

He never took any advantage of his position, ones there was an interview for the appointment of some posts in BHEL at Bhopal. There were many candidates who had come for the post. A young boy amongst them was asked to go in when his turn came and his name was announced. The member of the interview board asked for his CV., which was handed over by the boy, he was asked about his father's job details and name as a routine. The boy gave his father's name as Shri Lalbahadur

Shastri, and father's occupation as Prime Minister of India. The person asking questions was stunned and surprised that he was interviewing the son of the PM of his own country and was not informed about it. But when asked Mr. Shastri made it clear that as far as he was concerned his son was as ordinary as any other boy of the country and he should be selected or rejected on his own merits! I have never heard the incident like this a second time in my life.

He was the man who wanted to solve the food grain crisis during famine in his time as PM by giving up food ones a week on Monday to be able to feed all the country's population equally. "Fast every Monday" was his message in the form of a slogan! To give equal importance to the Army and farmers he came out with the slogan "Jai jaw an Jai Kisan." We had a hero in simplicity and sincerity at that time. The respect and love he earned from his people was tremendous. He was an example of a sincere, hard working and totally uncomplicated person hard to find.

To find a second category, there is one in India married to a girl from one of the most famous political family of India. He must have coined his plan at a very early stage in life. For convenience Let me call him Jack. So this Jack who is the son of an ordinary businessman became friendly to the girl during school days, when they were studying in private prestigious school of Delhi. The friendship continued after they finished the school. They remained in contact and then decided to get married. Jack's father was against the marriage but could not do anything about it because the mother was all in for it.

Jack's father had a business in fancy articles of brass and copper. His, must have been an ordinary business with reasonable income sufficient to run a small family, but Jack probably had different ideas. After getting married he entered reality business of buying and selling land and used his contacts after marriage.

His business prospered. While everything was going smooth and fine he lost his sister in some accident, then he developed some misunderstanding with his father. The father was found dead under mysterious circumstances. Jack shifted to Delhi after his father's death and is now living in Delhi. From the periphery this appears to be an ordinary story but there are so many stories circulating in the community about Jack, which draw attention towards something fishy going on. He has accumulated lots of wealth in short time. He makes plenty of foreign trips not really required for a normal ordinary business., and if one has to believe the stories, there is suspicion of smuggling on him. Why I mentioned this story here is simply to prove my point that the person who sells his conscious to devil can probably indulge into lot of weird activities and amass riches and materialistic comforts. He is a good topic of speculation and juicy gossip on the media. To me Jack appears to be a dubious character who indulges into all sort of activities to serve one aim that is to accumulate wealth and power.

According to me such type comes as the type of human beings who have no conscious, no fear of not doing anything wrong and they are usually without any fear of God or religion.

There are some persons who are open to doing any criminal activity without a hitch. They are more advanced in their criminal attitude. The devil of their persona is more alert than the God in their hearts. They rejoice in adopting a criminal carrier and spend their lives thriving looting, fooling molesting and even murdering for some gain. These are sort of psyches, which are also part of any human society anywhere in the world. I am certain they do not have any religious or Godly binding in their minds. The only emotion attracts them is extremes of selfishness. Such people can be dragged into doing any crime to serve their selfish goals.

They do not need a family, they do not care for affection and are like vagabonds in their dwellings. The people involved in drug smuggling, or those who are famous for illegal activities can be the examples.

There is a third type, who has let the devil overpower their minds, not because they enjoy, but because they are unhappy for not having enough of what they want. They do not know how and what to do, to get enough money and to fulfill their needs and wishes they seek out the source. Such persons are easy prey to the hunting sharks of the crime world. It is unfortunate that when the materialistic needs and physical pleasures become prime needs of any individual than conscious, God and religion lose their importance. The only attraction of life for a person of this mentality is money, wealth and power. The never ending greed never leaves the person. Drug mafias and Dons of the crime world are examples of the same. In eastern part of the world a person known as Daud Ibrahim and his partner known as chhota Shakil are quite well known for their activities, there are so many juicy stories about them in India and Pakistan. They sprang up in the world of crime from India and then expanded their territory to Pakistan and Dubai. Monetary and material prosperity with flavor of fear and torturous activities made them prosperous in their game to rule. The question still remains that do they have the satisfaction of leading the life of peaceful security of mind, of the type of respect they command by creating fear, are they happy in whatever they possess?

Having lots of wealth in the form of lands, houses, gold, vehicles, and army of assistants whom you may not trust! If this is the true happiness in life, then they are successful!

This attempt of mine to try and classify human beings into different categories is for understanding which can lead us to explain why we have so many variety of people in the universe who are involved in different type of unpleasant activities. Why there are those who love destruction and wars. Who force the quiet and satisfied happy ordinary people into a war like situation. Why do certain people want to rule the world through fear, and still shout the name of God while involving in unsocial activities. They are other name of destruction with a religious tag attached to their organization. These organizations thinks that to rule the world fear and power are very important. I do agree that these are fearful people out to spread destruction, misery, poverty and unhappiness in the world. They are successful in causing worry and concern to all who can understand. If it is the way to please God then in what way the world will survive!

26/11 is a date we can't manage to forget. On this day in the year 2009, terrorists attacked Mumbai. They created havoc on the Bombay central Railway station; they destroyed the famous Taj hotel. There were so many casualties of the common civilians and policemen. The country shivered with shock. It was a human tragedy of magnanimous nature for no possible and sensible reason. The young boys who were responsible for this calamity were trigger happy youths who were brainwashed for doing it and they kept shouting Allah Allah. It was a clear indication of certain sick minds, who think that they can spread their religious beliefs and philosophy by creating fear in the minds of simple, ordinary, and innocent people of the world. Of course they were successful in creating fear, which was like being attacked by wild animals even when one is feeling safe in one's own home. But does it mean that people will bow down to their demands and opinion because they are afraid? If that is what the understanding a terrorist organization gives to its followers then, is it not a fallacy created by a sick mind?

India recently suffered the Pathankot attack. We lost our officers and soldiers. We still have not recovered from the pain. Our peace loving country is a regular target of terrorism through the neighborhood country. I am sure every Indian and every human being is worried about it. Unfortunately there is no respite. There are some people who think that this is the only way they can please their God, they also claim that whatever they are doing is the most sacred work for God.

Killing innocents, burning schools, attacking and killing schoolchildren, can these actions be appreciated as the actions to please the God? If it is correct then is there a God in reality who is happy with all these horrible destructive activities? Or are these a group of very sick individuals who don't know what they are doing?

It seems all this ruckus is created by these mischief mongers because they have to take revenge from the people of different countries for God only knows what? The whole world is suffering, innocents are killed and tortured for no faults, and dear enemies of the world rejoice by opting different cruel methods of torturing and killing. Molesting raping and enslaving women is their favorite pass time and entertainment. All this is done to please God. One wonders what could be the religion of God who promotes such vulgar and senseless people to power, to insult, punish disrespect women and innocent children some time back there was a story presented on TV. It was the story about a Syrian girl. She belonged to a minority tribe of Syria. She was abducted by the terrorist organization active there. The girl appeared to be in her early twenties. She addressed the conference of generalists, she narrated her story. The way she was tortured beaten by the terrorists, she was forced for sex, and threatened with consequences if she did not compromise. It was so difficult to watch the whole thing.

All the time these people keep shouting Gods name, yet it seems that in their heart the emotion like sympathy and kindness is totally absent. They are settling their revenge for God or from God is only known only to themselves. What have the common people of the world done to them for which they are seeking revenge. A settling of scores from young innocent girls, from innocent kids whom they have dragged into the world of terror. Converted them to suicide bombers.

In Iraq there was Saddam Hussein, he ruled the country as a dictator. When one thought about Iraq during his rule, it was a country which had to dance to his tune. There must have been many simple civilians who succumbed to the pressure of his leadership and lived unhappily. That is the basic character of a human being, but the flames of rebellion was never extinguished. Saddam himself might have lived in luxury of physical comforts of a materialistic world, but he was never secure. The whole world knows his fate; I do not think anyone could have felt sorry for whatever he faced in the end. Unfortunately there is no end to the people of this thinking that by forcing their wishes on the weaker part of human society they are making world a better place to live. The twin brother of dear God appears to live in their hearts!

10

How will you adjust to the idea of a person whom you have trusted for a long time, shared your most sensitive secrets just feel easy in mind and heart, because you put him at a pedestal much higher than you could think. Then all of a sudden suddenly you realize that the one so important and respectful to you has done something so silly and degrading, that suddenly he comes tumbling down flat and gives the feeling of being a Lowly cheapest person you could not dream him to be. The shock will be unbelievable and the after effects will be like you yourself have been slapped hard on your own cheek.

Well something like this I saw happening to Uma, my dear friend. She was a great admirer of A God man who was called Bapu (father) by his followers. Uma came to visit... me while I was in Delhi. After some casual talk she told me that this time her coming to me is with a very important purpose. She has thought and thought and decided to take Deeksha from Bapu ji who is coming to Delhi for his discourses from next day onwards. The reason to receive the deeksha from Bapu was that he was a well known Saint of Hindus and according to Uma's thinking, if you don't have a Guru it's impossible to attain moksha after your death.

I was irritated and amused both simultaneously, because I had never thought of Guru and Deeksha so important to attain moksha or nirvana, also I had counted this particular activity almost a type of foolishness. Any effort from my side to convince Uma to forget this was not met nicely by her. She was more or less a blind follower of Bapuji whose discourses she meticulously followed on TV. When I tried to explain to her my view on these Bapuji type of people who are always engaged in dramatically trying to attract simple persons into a pseudo religious web, she snubbed me. I was not much surprised at her reaction. My friend is the type who gets her religious feelings mixed up with her belief that these so called saints can never do any wrong. So when she was determined to go for Deeksha I had nothing more to say. After all simple suspicion is not enough to prove one guilty. So I adopted the line of convenience for me and told her that I will provide her the car and the driver to go, but I will not go with her personally. She did not like it but had to agree.

On the day Bapuji was in Delhi, Uma Got ready much before the time of discourse and left the house. I instructed my driver to escort her properly and take care. Thus Uma left home to get her Deeksha.

She came back quite late in the evening when I had started getting worried if I had committed a mistake by sending her alone with the driver. As she came inside the house I was prepared to jump at her out of frustration that why she did not phone me. But when I looked at her face I decided to be quite and listen to what she had to say.

She was upset; she had not eaten or drank anything since she left. She told me that there was a huge crowd to see and meet Bapuji. People were paying donations amounting to thousands of rupees, just to have glimpses of Bapuji. It was impossible for her even to enter the camp area. Ultimately she gave up and returned back. She was upset that she could not get what she aimed for, I was happy for the same.

After four or five years of this incident, the news about Bapuji's ashrams in different states of the country started filtering in. There were reports of Many illegal activities going on in these ashrams, from drugs, money laundering, mishandling of kids murders of two of the inmate children's of the ashram was reported. There were also reports of Bapu and his son being involved in sexual assault of young females residents of the ashram. These ashrams were constructed on the style of luxury hotels with big luxurious bedrooms having cameras implanted in them. there were private swimming pools, pharmacies with many mysterious drugs in their store.

The irregularities and illegal activities going on in these ashram came as a big shock to the followers of Bapuji, not only Bapuji his son was also involved in these criminalities. On television in news the videos of both son and father dancing and singing were played. The whole country was feeling the pinch of shame by what these two did. They were ultimately arrested and put behind the bars. The inquiry was started? Though there were few who refused to believe that there most respected and loved Bapuji and his son had been party to so many crimes. They even went ahead by agitating against his arrest on the streets not only in one, but in many cities of India. On the plea of making ashram Bapuji had acquired land on illegal basis also, so when these facts were proved to be true after investigations many of the ashrams were demolished.

Bapuji's son hid himself when police started the process for his arrest. He kept running from one place to another for quite some time, he went to the extent of adopting fake personality too, but was ultimately caught. Now both father and son are in jail, and inquiries are going on against them.

When I met Uma after this Incident of Bapuji and his son she was very embarrassed. She expressed her sorrow about being so stupid and felt great full that she did not get involved with such people simply due to her good luck. We simply laughed it out.

Bapuji proved to be an expert conman and actor to be able to fool so many people for such a long time? He had developed very good connections with the people who belong to higher places in society and who used to support him and help him.

I have seen more of these babas, who very cleverly use their skills to fool people and enjoy good luxurious life at the cost of poor and innocent people. Who could be blamed?

If a person is prepared to be fooled? There is one who still comes on TV and holds regular shows! He sits on a throne like chair while presiding his meetings; he keeps his audience quite busy. The people in the crowd ask him questions like"

Babaji My business is not prospering?"

The Babaji smiles and asks him "Do you eat samosa?"

The man says "yes Baba ji."

Babaji says "Ok, from tomorrow, for one month, have samosa for breakfast every day, you will find improvement in business."

Another man asks "Babaji my son is not getting married"

Babaji smiles and says "Tell your son to keep his head on the window side of the room and sleep on the left side of the bed."

Babaji what do I do so that my wife listens to me?

Babaji smiles and says "wear yellow shirt with blue stripes and a black pant and eat pan regularly."

Many such reckless sessions of Baba and his followers go on. Hundreds of man and women happily attend these.

They do not see any foolishishness in this type of gatherings. They love to be deceived and fooled. What can be the reason for such faith?

I read somewhere that this particular Babaji is guilty of murdering his own father. He was in jail for his crime. After being released he disappeared for few years, and then resurfaced in his new avatar, and now he is prospering in his new business as awatari Baba!

Still the question remains unanswered that why people have so much faith on these pseudo saints. Can we blame the blind faith. Is any religion related to blind faith, or the fear of God, or expectation of some miracle in the life of a person who follows these criminals and fans their ambitions?

To a very great extent these pseudo saints are responsible for giving a political flavor to the religion at least in India. They are not only Hindus who encourage these people they are also found amongst Muslims and Christians or any faith. It is sad but very true. A keen observer can always find them out after one or two meetings. Only one has to keep the eyes open and senses alert. Those who want to create disturbances in the society do not care about the reason for doing so. It's not necessary that they should be trigger happy terrorists. These subtle quality mischief makers are more dangerous as they are hard to be recognized and difficult to be caught. They live as friends with us, though they are not friends, they pose as well wishers though they hardly ever wish well to anyone excepting themselves. The people who are self-centered are like this. They like to hoard, hide and increase their assets to unlimited extent, without realizing that it's impossible for them to utilize all this wealth collected by them ever in their life time. Such people can be called as curse for any society. or subtle terrorists. Black marketeers, money launderers, those involved in drug dealings and black money all belong to this category.

The other important fact is that unless we have confidence that what we do is right and know that it is not essential to be successful, comfortable and without problems always. There is no one who will not face success, and failure, happy moments as well as sad times in life. Even God, if decides to be born on this planet has to pass through all the phases in his life. I am taking the liberty of expressing this particular feeling because it makes me feel very strong when I think like this, and this thinking makes me more closure to my God.

11

It should not be taken as something absurd when I say that one of the most important cause of disturbing the peace in the world is politicizing the religions. The politicians are very shrewd people in the world. Under the false assurance of providing security, peace and happiness to the people of the part of the world they belong to, they squeeze away all the happiness and pleasure a common man gets through managing his own affairs.

In a society of multiple religious following by multiple different people of different views.

A Hindu will object to your praying without facing east, a Christian may come out with proper praying only in the church, and a Muslim might say unless you pray five time a day, you are not a proper religious person. It becomes a serious issue when a very hot discussion without leading to a proper solution takes place. Nobody wants their God to be ill-treated or disrespected, the fight breaks out and the most intelligent and practical person finds a way to peace by dividing all the religious parties into different groups hating each other, and the one who made them fight as a most sensible secular individual is the most ideal adorable person. The only thing he did was to create misunderstanding among the Hindus, Muslims and Christians and serve his own purpose of ruling the minds of all the three. Such pseudo secular individuals, with a carefully hidden motive of creating a thick vote bank, present themselves anywhere they feel a situation has arisen to serve their purpose.

It was a recent show like this in JNU campus of India. A group of students who got their incentive of participating in anti-national activity by criticizing and opposing the punishment given to some terrorists by the court. It was really painfully surprising that many of those who are well known political figures lined in the campus and held meetings with the students with a wrong understanding and sympathized with them.

The only reason for this attitudes appeared to be an opportunity to oppose and destabilize the government.

Any person who knows the history of our country will know that many of the present problems we are facing as a country are created by the wrong policy decisions by some leaders of the past. We can at least try and help those who are trying to rectify the mistakes of the past, instead of springing wrong ideas and supporting the wrong doers. Is it not shameful that even after seventy years of independence, and claiming to be one of the largest democracy of the world we elect our leaders on the basis of the family they belong to or the cast they belong to or the religion they follow?

Why do we make an issue of the food we eat, the temple we go to? Or why we call our God Bhagwan or Jesus or Allah or wahe Guru. Are we really tolerant of each other or just wear a fake mask of the sort.

In India we Hindus treat cows as sacred, we call her mother because we get so many benefits from her. Milk butter, ghee. Even her excreta is used for so many things. We believe that when the planet earth is in trouble it takes the form of a cow and goes to pray the God for suggesting a solution or helping in whatever way possible. The main reason is that cow is a very important animal that makes us take care of our needs in an economically sufficient way, it is a very intelligent animal and returns your affection in many folds, and hence it is treated as a family member and equated to mother. The main reason for Indians to respect the cow so much is because it caters for so many of their domestic needs, and we believe that all of us share the extension of our souls with God. So to treat another animal who is not a human, comes easily to us. Though I feel that not only cows, but the other domesticated animals too deserve the right to be treated with love dignity and respect.

There was a small video clip showing the torturous treatment given to piglets while killing them for meat. The process was so horrific that I could not watch it full. Even those who are fond of meat may feel like giving up eating meat if they happen to watch it. Similar treatment is given to many animals in the butcher houses to make the meat bloodless and probably tastier. The question is "Is it necessary to torture a poor animal, just to please the taste buds or are the human beings really human if they resort to such atrocities simply for eating something to enjoy the so called good taste?

There are two types of meat available in the market. One is called "halal" where the animal is killed a slow death by cutting it slowly after tying it. It is related to the religious sentiments of some. The other method is known as jhatka this method the animal is killed in one shot, I mean that it dies before it realizes. I personally do not agree for killing of any nature because I am a vegetarian. But I would like to know from those who understand the meaning of killing for eating.

But then to talk of the exploitation of the religious sentiments of one community and to try and flare up another community is so easy. The politicians from Muslim community of India found an opportunity to show their concern for their

Muslim brothers, and started holding meetings and declaring that cow meat is the cheapest source of nutrition, if they don't eat it they will starve. The agitations in both the communities became so inflamed that they started beating, looting killing, all the cruel and distasteful crude activities in the name of a poor animal who does not even know that she is the mother of one and essential food for the other community living in India, which is the secular country in the world.

Being a vegetarian it becomes difficult for me to understand someone's hunger which can't be satisfied without killing. I can justify the wild animals that have to kill or hunt to fill up their tummies and satisfy their hunger. It is also observed that these animals do not hunt unless their need to eat forces them to, or the very cold or very hot places where vegetation is deficient and even human being have to resort to killing. In a temperate climate where there is vegetation in plenty why one has to starve without killing. Why get so enraged to kill and destroy the others simply because they have different ideology about hunger!

All this happened because during the election time, politicians the people with a selfish rouge mentality will be able to Ancash some votes and remain in power.

In a village of UP in India an incident took place. A Muslim family who was a resident of the village for two or three generations, and had many Hindus as friends got some meat to be cooked for dinner. Everyone knows that meat is not a banned item in Muslim kitchen, but on that particular day some mischievous people went ahead to advertised that beef was being cooked in their house. Within minutes the agitated crowed got in front of their house, they killed the head of the family, badly wounded the son and the women folk. Later every one realized that talking about cow's meat for the dinner was wrong because the family had goat meat and not cow meat. The incident was some sort of settling some personal scores. It does not mean that action should not be taken against the criminals, but to give it a anti secular flavor is totally wrong.

The sympathetic politicians left every important job they were doing and dashed towards the village to shed their crocodile tears for the family with a sly intention of vote bank politics. It must have been a disgusting site. But a sight with a purpose or politicizing religious sentiments by politicians with moist eyes and sly smiles must have an amusing drama.

Such incidences have become frequent in India, the reason is purely political. Even when the politicians do not believe in any religion and any God. They want to sabotage the minds of simple people by playing religion card at the smallest opportunity they can grab and try to destabilize the government, even at the cost of nation's progress they do not stop. In an attempt to stabilizing there shaky position in political arena few of them even rushed to the neighboring country and openly asked for help, to destabilize the government in India!

That does not mean that religious politicking is not common in other countries. During very recent past there were thirty seven terrorists attacks in different countries all over the world. India is one of the countries which have lived under terrorist's threat constantly. We have survived Mumbai train blasts, we have survived attack twenty six eleven Taj hotel and other places in Mumbai targeted again, on our borders constant effort for infiltration is going on Kashmir, which is an integral part of India, has been a constant victim of trecharay. In the early nineties a motion to drive away the Hindus from Kashmir was started in a subtle but sure way by the some organizations. Their aim was simple, to create a Muslim majority on the land. Hindus are a race of over ten thousand years of civilization. Their growing civility and soft behavior made them more or less inclined towards cowardice. Added to this notion of civilization, in a properly developed morals of family it is obligatory that our male population of the society takes good care of the women and children of their family.

Growing atrocities and mental torture and the fear, that something obnoxious may happen to their families made them decide to leave the homeland. These people became refugees in their own country. They left their houses and a surroundings with meager equipment's to support them. The whole world was watching. But nothing could be done to help them. Even after more than twenty five years, these Kashmiri Pundits are waiting for a safe return to their homeland. At the same time the number of Muslim population of Kashmiris has increased. most probably with the inflow of Muslims from our neighboring country supported by militants and separatists.

Their next step which was obviously expected was to poison the mind of the people of India specially those who can be brain washed into sympathizing them to start the song of independence for Kashmir from India. It is sad but true that we Indians always treated Kashmir and its people as integral part of our country and culture. Without a hitch these separatists put their claim as if they are tremendously tortured by India and are treated as slaves or second class citizens. Forgetting completely that we recognized and agreed to honor and place a Kashmiri as our first priminister.

They also forgot the history of independence which clearly states that the than Maharaja of Kashmir willingly joined India.

Even if we go into the past and search, we find that Kashmir owns its name after Kashyap Rishi's name that was instrumental for its habitation, at a time few thousand years ago. At that time there was no sign of Islam. I definitely do not want to be disrespectful towards any religious sentiments of any community by saying this. But the fact remains that the claim of a reality which does not exist is falsehood. By cruelty, torture, and imposition one can't rule the mind and become supreme.

Still time has to prove the righteousness of thoughts and put justice in its rightful place.

Neither India has given up nor India has succumbed to any pressure. The whole world should be busy in finding a solution to this problem.

To me this appears to be a disturbance caused by politicizing the religion for personal gains. The earlier all the nations of the world understand it better it will be.

Various terrorists' organizations functioning in Islamic nations are also surviving on religious card. The people who join these organizations do so for many other reasons than God's wish. From a distance the money and facilities they offer to the youth appears very tempting. India has a huge poor population of Indians youths who have dreamt of the luxuries which appear beyond reach to them. The terrorist organizations take advantage of this fact and brainwash these young boys and girls of weaker and economically deprived groups in society by playing religious card. These boys and girls are contacted through Internet and are shown the dreams of what they will achieve, that also for serving the God by punishing those who are nonbelievers, all this simply by promoting the religion and punishing the people who do not believe in God. These young boys and girls are probably the victims of their own innocence and they get carried away by the talk of those who are experts in their ways to influence them. Many of these youngsters start realizing their mistake of leaving their home and going to the foreign land in search of better life, but by then they get completely enslaved by the bosses of the groups. For them the only alternative remains is to do whatever they are asked to do or get tortured or get killed. Some of them who are able to run away from such places have most horrible stories to tell. I know that God who exists in the heart and mind of a human being, and the God who takes care of the world and the people and all who inhabit ate it will never want any of His followers to behave in the way the people of these organizations behave. He will not like any one of his followers to perform cruelties like beheading innocents for creating terror in the heart of people, or to convert little children into suicide bombers, or to expose young girls and women to molestation, beating and raping. All this and then chanting the God's name while performing these atrocities. Should this be treated as the politicizing the religion or not is another issue but for sure any religion is bound to get a ting of dirt with such activities.

When India was struggling to become a free country, all the Indians of all religions existing in India were participating in the freedom struggle. The leaders who lead the struggle for freedom were Mahatma Gandhi who was promoter of non-Violence. There were others who did not believe that freedom was possible without violence. Subhash Chandra Bose was most prominent amongst those. Then there were some Muslim leaders, they were Maulana Abul Kalamazad, Abdulgaffar Khan and Mohd Ali Jinnah. They all struggled together, there might have been difference of opinion amongst some them, but religion did not play any major role till the end. Then when it became apparent that it will not be possible for Britain to hold on to India as its colony any longer, a game was played. Mohd AliJinnah, Jawaharlal Nehru was involved in the game with the Viceroy who was representing the Government of Britain and the Queen.

The religion card was a successful move, politicization of religion lead to breaking the country into Hindustan and Pakistan. About thirty thousand people were displaced. So many were massacred for no fault of theirs but the fact that they were Hindus in a Muslim dominated area or Muslims in a Hindu zone. The wounds have not healed, probably never will. In this process of partition both Hindus and Muslims suffered. God did not or could not help in the end a relationship of hate was established between the two nations and it still continue.

Pakistan is the nation from where the trend of Islamic nations has started; India declared itself a secular country. Many Muslims did not migrate to Pakistan and became the part of the mainstream of the nation. It has majority as Hindus, then Muslims, Sikhs, Christians and parses as minority religions. People learned to live together and were respectful of each other's religious sentiments. They participated in each other's festivals, celebrating the individual festivals of any religion with great enthusiasm, but the politicians with polluted mind saw to it that common men and women do not live in peace and harmony, so they come out with tricks which can be used as ready inflammable material. Religion and castes are the best weapons for war of this nature with very high potential for guaranteed success. The indigenes politics of India started suffering from the day one of independence due to these politicians with polluted mind. Gandhi's suggestion that congress should be dissolved after freedom was neglected by many. India suffered may not be in silence but in ignorance. Ignorance which was born of illiteracy and ignorance and blind faith in the political party which was Gandhi's child. Even though insincerity was obvious in the group people of India ignored it. They kept supporting the party to come in power again and again. The congress and its image kept deteriorating, sixty years was too much of time to be fooled but it happened due to extremely tolerant Indian society, supported by the illiteracy and ignorance.

I have grown from childhood to old age witnessing Pakistan playing religious card to create disturbances in India. After partition the number of Hindus who stayed back has reduced drastically. Those who find it difficult to come to India are treated callously.

To a very great extent politicizing the religion and faulty education was the cause. Almost three generations suffered. Fortunately the circumstances have started changing now. Indian youth are waking up and voicing their opinions wherever needed. It seems God is listening again!

12

Even at the moment of conception, destiny plays its role. Out of millions of sperms one is selected for fertilization. At that moment the fate decides whether the growing fetus is going to be a male or female. By the time the growing ball of cells becomes around sixteen cells in numbers, it is ready to implant itself in the uterine wall, at about the same time the cells which have to develop into the individual and the cell which had to help the individual to develop are classified. The discipline of the almighty does not stop here. Each single cell in the animal pole is tagged to perform a particular job of participating in the making a specific part of the individual. So much accuracy and so much precision are possible only with extremely careful watch by nature, it is astounding but true. I have tremendous gratitude that I could understand this miracle, and thank God for it. I have also understood that each cell that divide and re divides to form multiple cells of an organ, tissue, or any other part of the body is fed with the directions of its future role in the formation of the body in making inside a womb. Howsoever complicated it might appear but the direction of the director is so accurate and discreet. That's the creator we all like to call him God and feel that he is our protector and guide too.

The second aspect of creation which is equally important cannot be seen. It has to be experienced. Though it is equally active from the stage one of creation, its invisible presence is responsible to a very great extent for the recognition of the type of personality the individual is going to possess. That's where the sensitivity and emotions enter the scene. The touch, the taste, the smell, the sight, and the hearing all play the part. Excess or absence, of any one of these can give birth to the emotions which no words can describe, but it can be felt. What will be the resulting outcome will be experienced by those who are present in the surroundings as humans or non-humans as refined or crude individuals. The fully formed Individual is the result of treatment the time and circumstances give to the this individual, to be a demon or a saint.

Nature is averse to extravagance of any kind. We may not be able to perceive this in its true sense but the ultimate result of anything happening always tells us. For example, all of us know that everything present in the universe, big or small, ugly or good looking, living or dead has to be treated with respect and care plus love. Neglect any one of these emotions and you will have a problem at hand. Use any one of these emotions in abundance; again you will have a problem knocking on you. Reduce or make deficiency in amount of any one of these emotions and you will have a problem to face.

In the society of humans divided into groups by using religion, we say treat everyone with respect and care. Do we really do it? Question might appear absurd, but I Think it's important question we have to keep asking to ourselves from time to time. If we want a healthy society.

There are two individuals needed to start a family. A man and a woman. Both of them are provided with capacity and qualities of different nature to care and need of the family. Where command, discipline, and exposure to the rough outer world are needed man is the most suiting individual.

When it comes to compassion, caring and love, woman is the best. Unfortunately when the life progresses and circumstances change, the world's ideals starts disappearing. Woman forgets compassion care and love and the man becomes imposing and crude dominating and uncivilized. The pleasant harmony starts crumpling and the family, does not look heavenly. If the families break the society becomes a skeleton monument of a once lively existence. It is neither good nor proper to blame only men or only women for a crashed culture. It's a joint attitude of the two parallel supporters of a structure.

Things happen if in society of humans a group forgets the value of woman in the family. The men start thinking that she should be treated as lesser human. She should not be given freedom of expression, and should be only treated as an object for physical pleasures to be enjoyed and discarded, what will happen to the heaven we call family. It's a fact which can't be over looked. In India where we treat women with respect. She is put on a high pedestal as a Goddess, as a mother, as a loving sisters or a dear wife.

Where will a man go at the end of the day, without the presence of a compassionate loving and caring and passionate woman? What will a woman do in a house without a rough, but commanding and demanding, protective and loving man, who will give her the world she wants and deserves? There are religions of the world who have forgotten that without the man and woman being together any society whether it is humans or other animals cannot survive. They are on the verge of destruction. They probably can't see or feel the need to improve. Instead they feel that to convert the whole world into a demonically strong and hellish place to live. Hell might not appear hellish to them and demonic ways may give them a sense of being all powerful and capable. They may forget that it takes two to make a fairyland or a monster 's kingdom but the truth remains that whatever you want you will make. heaven or hell but ultimately it's you and you only who will have to live in it.

If as members of a society of humans, we feel that something has to be done to stop from it becoming a hell; we have to think hard for achieving that goal. We have to know that the force of the devil is very strong somewhere in the world. Not only it is strong but it's increasing rapidly, with a dangerous speed. The nations are getting destroyed, innocent lives are in danger and glimpses of disaster are nearing the horizon. What is the solution, whether there is one or not has to be decided fast, really fast.

There are two obvious ways to check the destructive ways of this demonic group one is to destroy the destructor by force. Many countries are trying it. How far they have been successful? Is a debatable question. The other thing is that forceful destruction has to go on and on till you are hundred percent sure that you Have succeeded. How long it will go on nobody knows. Then to adopt a destructive attitude towards any one we consider destructor by many groups of people jointly is possible or not is also questionable. The capacity of the different nations in this respect has to be assessed. If all the sensible part of the world will join together is another question.

To opt for destroying all who go on a killing mission is not so easy. Kill a lot and another is born. It's an unending process. To Catch some, treat them back into sensibility, gain their confidence and convince them that what they were doing was wrong and against the ethics of any religion, the leave them into their own group for detoxification of their group. This appears to be a theoretical possibility.

The second option is to control the psyche of the destructors through psychological means in a massive drive. This is possible but the success is not guaranteed. It's an old method tried successfully in olden times, but even if the thousands of us concentrate on the target i.e. The minds of the monsters, into influencing them to behave the way we want them to do. Will it be possible, will we be able to break the walls of lie and deception created by them in their minds. The distant psychological therapy as is given in Japanese art of healing is very popular in India, it is called "Reiki." The healers send their healing from distance.

"In the End"

All I can think and say is that irrespective of our feelings about our God, in whatever religion we follow, the thought that we have Him for our guidance, protection and happiness is a thought which makes us secure. Still as animals of a superior order we don't fail to perform atrocities of various order to prove that we know better, in the long run our intelligence turns out to be our worst enemy. We may belong to any group. Community, or race, but to establish our own superiority over each other we never leg behind. To prove we are better in the language we speak, the feats we can perform as warriors, our color, our mannerism, even the negotiations to achieve certain goals, We are the best, should never be forgotten. This leads to frictions and fights.

The result is that everything done or created by some other group turns out to be defective according to our own standard. Then we don't want to lose time to impose ourselves, our ideas to the crowed we consider inferior to our group and ideology. Thus starts the friction between people of different casts and creeds, colours and language, religions and customs and even different sexes.

So many wars have been fought since the time immemorial, for different ethics and ideologies, different races and religions. Different groups won them at different time in different situations, we go according to the history or the stories told to us about these wars and decide about who was wrong and who was right. Majority of the time the group of people who lost the war are labeled as wrong doers. It appears right because those who are winners usually can't be projected as wrong. In Ramayana written by Goswami Tulasidas he clearly says that 'samarath ko nahi dos gusai' meaning the stronger person is always right.

If I think on these lines, and analyze the situation in our various societies it is very clear. Sometimes a devilish organization is supported and raised by political societies as has happened in many Muslim countries to serve some political purpose and later they are targeted as anti-socials or terrorist organizations. Rise of Saddam Husain and Gaddafi are burning examples of such people and Osamabin Laden is another one. It was easy to provoke these people due to the conditions they were facing in their society, extremes of religious fanaticism made them easy targets.

To fight about the faith is a common practice. Secularism is a thought totally unsuccessful, whatever we think or say when it comes to religions almost everyone gets stuck somewhere in the process of accepting the ideology different to their own. Then the politicizing of religion in a secular country is so closely related to vote bank that our political stalwarts can go to any limit to secure their position in their political arena to fan even the wrong ideas and customs of a minority religious groups or communities.

The incidences which could be ignored by the media are highlighted to magnanimity on provocations of political pundits. The common citizen is provoked and is forced by this game to get involved. The normal actions for the progress of the society and nation are brought to standstill. To top this all the religious heads and leaders along with politicians and media persons join group discussions and gain footage in their fields through this drama. The citizen who is a common man or woman loses their peace and become distrustful of every body and anybody thus become unhappy. Under these circumstances Gods of all religions just watches with no solution.

Is it possible for us human beings who belong to different religions and communities to make certain rules we should follow peacefully, the way we have learnt since birth and be happy with our own privacy and security in which we can pray and enjoy being in company of The God we have learned to trust and love.

There is no most perfect or most superior or inferior method of worship. The worshippers follow their own trends and feel happier that way. It's simple this way. There are many examples to prove this statement. Different methods of worship in different religions are proof enough. In Hindu places, we want the worshippers to enter the temple without shoes 'in churches it's just opposite, you have to be properly dressed with shoes on. Plus decent dress code. There are places of worship in Jews where non-Jews are not allowed. There are other places where non Hindus are not allowed, and then there are places where women are not allowed. It does not appear to be the work of God who will say no to any of his worshippers to be discarded in this fashion. It's definitely created by humans with faulty understanding about the God.

Imposing a different way of worship on others is a way to cause disruption in life of others; this is a very harmful trend and should never be practiced.

In any community the woman's position should be secured and respectful. It is not possible for anyone to ignore his or her first teacher, guardian and friend. In the families where this rule is followed peace and order persists. Children are well brought up and mutual respect towards one and all is appreciable. These families can easily be rated as very civilized and worth following as exemplary. In case the circumstances are opposite, anxiety, fights, deceptions and all sorts of activities which can cause disturbances in the family become imperative.

Where man holds the position in a family as head, the woman has to be with him to support him in the right way; anywhere if this rule is not followed with sincerity descent becomes imperative.

This phenomenon is already seen in the communities who are breaking the rule and ill-treating their girls and women.

Self-respect and caring is the main quality, to be possessed by one and all. We may belong to any religion and culture, as far as possible we have to learn that our religious sentiments for the God are our own and very private for our families. They should not be open for public. This privacy about religious feelings and emotions has to be carefully followed by the citizens of a secular country like India. more so if we the citizens do not want the political parties trying to make issues about anything and everything concerning religion and cast.

We have to be extremely particular as educated and sensible people, to not to let our religion become a tool to be played in a dirty game by politicians and making us enemies of each other.

Living and behaving like a true human being is the best attitude, if that is done the world will again become a beautiful and loving place to live.